DOMESTICATED
JESUS

DOMESTICATED
JESUS

HARRY L. KRAUS JR.

P.O. BOX 817 • PHILLIPSBURG • NEW JERSEY 08865-0817

Library of Congress Cataloging-in-Publication Data

Kraus, Harry Lee, 1960-
  Domesticated Jesus / Harry L. Kraus, Jr.
     p. cm.
  ISBN 978-1-59638-185-8 (pbk.)
  1. Jesus Christ--Person and offices. 2. Jesus Christ--Example. 3. Christian life.
I. Title.
  BT203.K73 2010
  232'.8--dc22
                                        2010009602

CONTENTS

Introduction   7
Domesticating the Lord of the Universe

1. I Don't Want to Grow Up   17
   Domesticating Jesus by My Own Immature Faith

2. On Pedestals and Plastic Smiles   25
   Domesticating Jesus by Acting Christian

3. The Bigness of the Real Jesus   33
   Domesticating Jesus by Underestimating His Power

4. A Very Big Gospel Plan, Part 1   43
   Domesticating Jesus by Wallowing in Guilt

5. An Unpredictable, Miraculous Jesus   55
   Domesticating Jesus in a Safe, Scientific Box

6. A Very Big Gospel Plan, Part 2   63
   Domesticating Jesus by Underestimating the Power of the Gospel

7. "But Whatif?"   75
   Domesticating Jesus by Our Worry

8. Losing Control   85
   Domesticating Jesus in Our Anger

9. The Security of Sameness   95
   Domesticating Jesus by Not Trusting the One Who Holds the Future

10. Yawning in the Presence of a Mighty God   109
    The Reason We Are Complacent in Sunday Worship

11. Down, but Not Out   129
    Domesticating Jesus by Hiding Our Sin

12. Grace Is the Key to Overcoming Nagging Addictions   137
    Domesticating Jesus by Walking in Our Own Strength

13. The Gospel of the Domesticated Jesus   153
    It's Really All about Me, Isn't It?

14. When Hope Falters   169
    Discouragement When Jesus Is Small

15. Short-circuiting the Flow of Grace   175
    Domesticating Jesus by Our Bitterness

16. Fire-escape Christianity   185
    Domesticating Jesus by Living by My Rules

17. Incarnation   199
    The Most Amazing Domestication of All

INTRODUCTION

Domesticating the Lord of the Universe

"DJ." I MIGHT AS WELL call him this, because effectively I've reduced the Creator and Master of the universe down into a concept so small I've nicknamed him. Domesticated Jesus. It's a horrible name really, and my use of it hardly reflects his worth. But to say it, to write it here is so shocking that perhaps that's the point after all. What we're doing, unconsciously to a large part, is to bring down what is huge, wild, and untamable and repackage him so that we can function.

To come to grips with reality will mean I have to change, open my eyes, and come to terms not only with his greatness but also with my smallness, and that's the grind. Sin has done this to me, landed me in this spot, and so I'm vowing forever to fight this ironic switch, the one that's been with mankind since a snake convinced my ancestors that they could be like God. That switch, of course, is the essence of sin. Louie Giglio is a talented speaker with a passion to see Jesus glorified in the lives of our youth. I heard him explain sin as anything that makes a big God small and makes my small self big. Surgeons like that kind of bottom-line thinking. Let's get real and honest about

7

our personal dirt. I'm talking about the way I make myself big. And that is the definition of the "s" word: sin.

And in the process, I've domesticated the Almighty.

Tamed him. Advised him.

Put him in a box. Fenced him into a safe pasture.

Expected him to function like a divine vending machine.

I like that because I get to be in control or at least sit on a deluded cushion of mental comfort where I've convinced myself that I'm in the driver's seat. The truth is, every time I come face-to-face with just a fraction of the reality of who Jesus is, I realize just how horribly weak my version of him has become.

And that sickens me. Shocks me.

And it should.

I've started writing this on a memorable day. It's Easter. A day we celebrate a God who became man, died, and beat death at its own game. I love Easter. At least for a day (or a few moments for some of us) the veil seems to lift, and we acknowledge with our lips that God himself is with us. Alive. Seeing all. *With us.* Desiring to interact with us. And not just to hear me speak. Intimacy purchased with blood spilled beneath a Roman cross.

Easter is a fitting day to begin a new project like this one because it carries with it the hope that reality may rise in my heart as certain as the resurrection that we celebrate.

Right now I'm sitting in an African airport waiting to board my plane. It's shameful in a way that I've trivialized this most precious of Sundays for something as mundane as travel. Is this even more evidence of the pathology within me (and in all of the church), bringing down the big and making large the small?

A few moments ago my wife eyed my brown journal with a look of suspicion. I should tell you that we're off on a trip to celebrate twenty-five years together. That's twenty-five years with a great deal of "putting up" on her part. Medical school, surgical residency, giving up life in America because of my missionary dreams. So maybe her suspicion is deserved. This is supposed to be a vacation, not a working retreat.

I faced her. Honesty has worked wonders for our first twenty-five years. "I'm starting a new book."

She's heard this line a dozen times from me, each time the truth. "Fiction or nonfiction?" she asked.

"Nonfiction."

"*The Close Second*," she said, referring to a conversation we'd had earlier in the day. "Hope," Pastor Crumley said, "runs a close second to love." (Remember 1 Corinthians 13? "Faith, hope, and love abide, these three; but the greatest of these is love.") I had told her that *The Close Second* would be a great title for a book on hope.

"Nope," I said. "*Domesticated Jesus*."

She didn't hesitate. "I don't like it. It makes Jesus sound effeminate."

I don't like it either, and that's the point.

To even associate the name above all other names with a word like *domesticated* is offensive to the delicate Christian ear.

If this offends you, good. It should. I hope that my use of this distasteful title will shock me (and you) into a healthy pondering of just what we're doing in this life we've identified (perhaps too generously) as *Christian*.

So how have I come to associate a word like *domestic* with Jesus?

I'll state the obvious. Domestic. Tame. The unruly is gone. Away with unpredictable behavior. Wildness is only used in the past tense here.

The first animals that were domesticated were done so for milk. Mmmm. Keep those cows contained. Train them to stay in line. Hold still . . . and give me just what I want. Every day. Twice a day in most cases.

We've trivialized him. Have you seen the cool new milk commercials? The slogan "Got milk?" is emblazoned on TV screens and billboards, reminding us of our need for a nutritious beverage. Given our culture, perhaps the spillover was inevitable. I've seen the T-shirts proclaiming a spiritual parody of the ads: "Got Jesus?"

Wow. As if we can begin to compare our need of a Savior to milk.

If an animal is domesticated, it is here to serve me. My needs are central. Of course, this might not always appear to be the case at first glance. I once heard someone ask what an alien would think after landing on earth for the first time in the center of an American city park. Dog owners leading around their little precious fur-bearing gems and picking up after their every little indiscretion. The alien might ask, "Who has domesticated whom?"

I'm going to ask you a favor. Indulge me while I seek to explore the ways that I have domesticated Christ. Yes, yes, I can hear your protests, and believe me, they are my own. Jesus Christ cannot be domesticated!

I understand that. And my point is simple. While Christ cannot be tamed, I have effectively done just that, but only in my head. I domesticate him in the way I think about him, letting him into my life, but only so far, until my control is threatened and, in effect, I send him back to his room.

When you domesticate an animal, you place limits on its location. You fence it in so that it can serve you. Have I not done this in my attitudes about Christ? Have I not invited the most holy, powerful, creative entity in the universe into my life and then relegated him into a slot so that he can participate in my life when it is most convenient to me or when I am hungry?

Some of you are offended already. It is not my purpose to spit on the image of Christ. My purpose is honorable; it is to exalt him, to find him as the grand treasure that he is and to challenge myself (and you along the way) to see him every day, to a greater extent, in reality.

To do that, I must peel away, layer by layer, the belittling mental images that have clouded my vision like a mature cataract blocking away the brightness of the sun's rays. I promise to step on my own toes first, and if I tramp on the feet of God's family, it is with the hope that we may discover and savor the wonder of all that Jesus is.

I am an honest seeker, and I invite you to sit with me and humor me as I extend this metaphor. My hope is that you will read these words as they are intended. I am no theologian unless you can stretch your mind to think of a Sunday armchair quarterback theologian of sorts.

Oh, I have years of biblical training to be sure, but I'm hardly qualified as a biblical authority. My expertise is in the area of medicine, surgery to be exact, and I'm sure a clinical aroma will seep into these pages before it's all been said. Perhaps more importantly, I've found myself drawn as a storyteller (and I believe God is doing the drawing in this case). So this is the platform in which I intend to explore this subject with you—as a fellow seeker, pained by my own failure to see Jesus as he really is, a clinician familiar with the pathology of human experience, and finally as a storyteller with a pen ready to illustrate our plight.

I write as a believer in Christ. This needs to be understood from the outset. I will borrow heavily from the New Testament, a book that is both authoritative and divine. Perhaps this is the stumbling block for many of you, one that must be overcome if we are to reach the same place together in the end. It is not my intention to validate this starting point. Many others far more qualified than I have written on the historical reliability of the Gospels and the Bible. I refer you to them to address these issues.

If you are not yet a believer in Christ (and here I use the term synonymous with true Christian, one who has placed his or her faith securely in Christ for salvation), then this book is a wonderful place to start, for the ultimate question for every person is this: *Who is Jesus?*

If you're not a Christian, I applaud you for even picking up a book with this title. Perhaps more likely, a well-meaning Christian friend shoved it into your hands. Consider this a safe place to begin an exploration. Here is your chance to find out what Christians really think without the I-know-all-the-answers nonsense. I'm an "insider" to the Christian movement. I grew up in the church and have spent years as a Christian missionary on foreign soil, so if anyone (outside of a seminary ivory tower) qualifies to offer an authentic opinion as to what we believe, I'm it. Some of what I say will apply mostly to Christians, so for that part, please assume the fly-on-the-wall mental posture and enjoy the fact that I'm trying to stir the pot and make Christians get real about what they believe or at least claim to believe. The world has seen enough phonies. I hope that this book can help you see that some of us are for real.

That said, I want to make something absolutely clear. A true judgment of Christianity should rest solidly on an investigation of Jesus himself, not on what I or any follower of his can say. We've certainly screwed up his message enough over the years and have proven that Christians are the biggest stumbling block to many sincere seekers.

If you are a Christian, then this book is also for you. My hope is to rattle the cage of your faith a bit, to challenge you to think critically about how much the Jesus you serve resembles the real deal, the Jesus of the Bible. I hope that you will think of this as a conversation with a friend, a fellow seeker, honest enough to ask tough questions. I am an imperfect fellow, stained from my own experiences, both good and bad. Think of me as a comrade in arms, nestled down with you in the same trenches of life, whispering together about some of the questions that have dogged humans from the beginning.

Here's my problem. I'm terrified of putting this down on paper.

There. I've admitted it. I am painfully aware of my shortcomings, both spiritually and intellectually. How is it that I possess the boldness to proceed into waters that scare me and threaten to derail my own faith?

Because I think we all have a similar, yet unspoken fear. And we need to get it out and talk about it. Christians don't have to hide and pretend there is no disconnect between our experience and what we see written in the pages of the Bible. We read stories of miracles, see a man who commanded waves and wind (and they obeyed!), took authority over demonic spirits, spoke breath into the dead, and we wonder, *Do I really know Jesus?*

If I have to be transparent (and I do or this project will fail, for the foundation of our relationship is that I'll be honest with you, and you, in turn, need to be honest with yourself), I'll admit that I'm terrified that if my eyes are opened someday to see everything in the light of truth, I will also see that the way I see the Jesus whom I claim as Lord is but a dim reflection of reality.

This fear is what drives me onward. *I want to know him.*

I'm afraid that I can never do justice in describing or explaining the majesty, power, and perfection of Jesus. That's the nature of human discussions, I suppose. No matter how high above my own experience I reach, I'll never be able to adequately pen the qualities of a perfect God. And so even my attempts to expose how I have domesticated Jesus will do just that: I'm bound to domesticate him further—to wrap him within pages of description implies that he is small enough to describe. To have humans speak of him, to write of him, implies that we can in some way wrap the human mind around him.

Of course, that's impossible.

And that is, in part, my point. It's what I want to challenge myself to see, and you to hear. I want to raise my own awareness of my sinful tendency to make the big small and the small big.

This is the essence of my working definition. I am domesticating Christ anytime my behavior reflects my belief in a saving Christ who is too small to handle my day-to-day problems of worry or anxiety. I am domesticating him anytime I wallow in guilt because, in essence, the power of the cross has been diminished in my thoughts. It has become insufficient to soothe my conscience.

Domesticating Jesus is so much more than just not recognizing his infinite power and falling on our faces in awe. He obviously doesn't reveal himself in his glory, at least not in his full glory, or I promise I'd never get out of a facedown posture (of course, I wouldn't survive a millisecond of his revealed glory, so even that statement is ludicrous). But these essays are about how I domesticate him every day in so many ways, in little things like doubt, anxiety, or fear about the future.

From the start I'll share my bias. Not one of us on this side of Heaven will ever really understand Christ in all his glory. But every one of us can make an effort to remove a few of the filters that have dimmed the true light and replaced it with something else altogether.

Bias number two: I don't have all the answers. If I accomplish my goal, you'll be asking more questions at the end of our time together than before. Questions, I believe, are the essence of living faith, an irony that has seemingly passed right over a large number of us as Christians. Don't think—just believe, we're told.

Hooey. I could use cruder terminology here, but here at the beginning of our time together I don't want to risk turning you away.

I seek freshness. Honesty. Transparency.

Maybe if I use this approach, we can link hands so to speak and take a baby step or two along a path toward a true Christianity. A Christian faith one notch purer than the one with which we started.

So pull up a chair, fellow traveler. Let's sit together to reason about a horrible thing that I've done.

I've domesticated the Lord of the universe.

1

I DON'T WANT TO GROW UP

Domesticating Jesus by My Own Immature Faith

MEET BOB. He's a lot like me (and you). Perhaps if I tell you about Bob, you'll find his trouble a bit amusing, and any lessons that Bob learns along the way can be ours also. Of course, there's the added benefit that you won't throw this book across the room quite so fast, 'cause I'm just talking about our friend Bob and not singling out anyone else by name. Got it?

Right.

Bob. Bob Christian. Thirty-four. One wife, Sally. Two kids, Bobby Jr. and Beth Ann. Bob and Sally met during college where he studied architecture and she got her bachelor's degree in nursing. They have a big house, a bigger mortgage, two cars, a wellness center membership; they play golf and tennis at a private club and dine out weekly at their favorite little country inn just outside of town. The children are in private school, although every fall Sally feels a little guilty that she doesn't have the energy to homeschool the kids. He's a Rotarian, and she is a member of a book club and shows their house (Bob's design, of course) on the home and garden tour every spring, an event that raises money for the pediatric unit at the county hospital. With their dual income, they've had a chance to vacation in Jamaica during the Michigan winter and take at least one snow skiing trip each of the last four years. They are planning a trip to Europe this summer after Bobby Jr.'s soccer camp.

Bob's partner is Muslim; his secretary is a Buddhist.

And, oh yeah, Bob's a Christian. At least that's the box he checked on the last census. They don't attend church like they used to. Bob always needs Sundays to sleep in. They write a check to the United Way every year and give their pocket change to Beth Ann to drop in a bell ringer's bucket for the Salvation Army.

They have no idea how today is going to change their lives. A jagged rip through the gentle fabric that has become their security is on its way.

But before I introduce you to the tragedy that is their appointed destiny, let me back up a bit. Just how did Bob and Sally come to call themselves Christian?

Bob was ten years old when he went forward at a revival meeting held in the First Baptist Church where his parents attended. That's when he "asked Jesus into his heart." Since that time, he's grown very little in his faith. In fact, other than holding steadfastly to the "once saved, always saved" doctrine that his father said is beyond debate, he knows little of the Bible at all. He prays with his family before dinner on the few nights a week that the family has time to sit together. Perhaps you know the prayer he uses. "God is great, God is good, now we thank him for our food." Sometimes they get Bobby Jr. to say the prayer. He says it so fast that the whole family has been known to laugh.

Bob learned most of what he knows about Jesus from his parents. While they were sincere, they were of the belief that since they took Bob to Sunday school, he would absorb everything he needed there. Time at home was for real-world learning, and unfortunately his parents failed to model an integration of the Christian faith beyond Sunday mornings.

Holidays were important to Bob's family as he grew up, and they even attended the Christmas and Easter pageant put on at their local church. But mostly Christmas was all about the gifts (and not *the gift*), and Easter was all about finding the large chocolate bunny that his mother would hide for him (after all, he was too Christian to believe in the Easter Bunny).

Bob's father was a product of the Great Depression, a lift-yourself-up-by-the-bootstraps sort of fellow. Quiet. Self-made. A man who rose from nothing to run a small chain of grocery stores that he sold last year to Food Lion. The real preaching that Bob took home from his father was an ethic of hard work, little play, and an honest day's wage for an honest effort. His father always told him, "If you do it yourself, you know it will be done right."

Is Bob a true Christian? He certainly thinks he is and would argue 'til he's blue in the face about theological issues about which he knows little.

But he's not a real Christian. How do I know?

Because I made him up. If he was a real person, I could honestly say that only God knows the heart. Jesus gave us some criteria for judging another's life by looking at the fruit, but he also made it clear in parables that there are tares among the wheat and that we might not find out who is real and who is phony until the harvest.

19

Bob is living under the delusion that repeating a prayer to ask Jesus into his heart was the only magic he needed to provide an escape from hell.

When crisis hits Bob's family, where is he likely to turn for help?

We will soon see.

An American Tragedy

Every day an American (and worldwide) Christian tragedy is played out in thousands of lives. So many have come to Christ, made an initial commitment with a child's understanding, and then stagnated. Sometimes the decision was real. Other times it was simply to please parents or a Sunday school teacher. Some, like Bob, hold earnestly to their salvation as if clutching a get-out-of-jail-free card if death sneaks up and surprises him or her early.

In a recent example of drivel coming from Hollywood, the protagonist of *Talladega Nights* prays to "Dear baby Jesus."

If only Hollywood's parody didn't strike so close to home.

Christians whose faith has remained infantile will rarely integrate their faith into the center of who they are. Christ is ornamental, a baby in a manger scene. Jesus is domesticated in their minds, because he's never grown up. More accurately, our understanding of his power, his glory, our understanding of grace and truth has been stymied far short of reality. It's a problem as old as the church. The writer of the book of Hebrews laments.

> About this we have much to say, and it is hard to explain, since you have become dull of hearing. For though by this time you ought to be teachers, you need someone to teach you again

20

the basic principles of the oracles of God. You need milk, not solid food, for everyone who lives on milk is unskilled in the word of righteousness, since he is a child. But solid food is for the mature, for those who have their powers of discernment trained by constant practice to distinguish good from evil. (Hebrews 5:11–14)

On Easter morning back when my boys were small, the three of them shared one bedroom. As I was taking call for the weekend, I needed to leave for the hospital, but I wanted to spend a little time reading to the boys about the significant event that we were celebrating before I went off to work. I read to them from a modern version of the Bible, telling the story of the resurrection. I read the section from the book of John where Peter and John entered the garden tomb. As I reached the end of the sentence, I raised my voice so that they would understand I was asking a fill-in-the-blank question. "They went into the tomb and they did not find the _____." I stopped and looked at my boys for the answer.

Without hesitating, my then-three-year-old yelled, "The eggs!"

I sighed. And laughed. My young son had the American version of Easter down pat.

Another Sunday morning when Sam was about the same age, he looked up at me during a church service and pointed at our pastor. "Is that God?"

To understand what happened next, you need a little background. Sam couldn't get his small mouth adequately around the word "girl." It always came out sounding like "grill."

I understood Sam's dilemma. I'm sure we had used the phrase "God's house" when referring to the church building. "No," I whispered. "God is not a man."

21

Sam's little face twisted with concern. A moment later, he had apparently figured it out but decided to confirm it with me. "He's a grill?"

We laugh at our children's understanding. We cherish every baby step, even when they stumble, because that's how *babies* are supposed to act and speak.

Unfortunately for Bob and for many in the church, the tragedy of growth failure is lost on them. They cling to a few infantile notions of faith and fail to see how it could be relevant to the important issues of day-to-day success and survival.

My children are now entering the age where they are leaving the nest for college. I remember my reaction at dropping my firstborn off at the U.S. Air Force Academy. Parents all around us were crying, hugging their sons and daughters before handing them over to Uncle Sam for basic training. Mothers were more verbal to be sure, but I saw plenty of fathers brushing back tears.

Joel stood under a sign that said, "Parents' Last Look," a placard that noted the separation point.

I reached for him one last time. Just the day before, it seemed, I had cradled him in my arms and rocked him to sleep. As he hugged me, he obviously didn't trust me not to make a scene. The message he gave me was clear: Don't cry. Let's be men about this.

"It's just summer camp, Dad," Joel said. "Summer camp." Knowing what was ahead, perhaps he was trying to convince himself.

I hugged him close and held back the emotions threatening to erupt.

Later, having watched him board a bus to be taken to the gold footprints (where the incoming basic cadets are taught how to stand at attention for the first time), I drove away in my rental car with the road blurring from my tears. For twenty-four hours after that until I boarded a plane and left Colorado Springs, the knot in my throat and the threat of tears were never far beneath the surface.

As hard as it is to let our children go, imagine our distress *if they never left home*. Worse yet, imagine if they never grew up at all. What would it be like to spoon-feed, dress, bathe, and diaper our children into their teens? Or twenties? Or for a lifetime?

Have I allowed my understanding of Christ's power, his grace, and his love for me to mature throughout my Christian life?

Over and over the writers of the New Testament compare our growth as Christians with the growth and maturation of our physical bodies. "But grow in the grace and knowledge of our Lord and Savior Jesus Christ" (2 Peter 3:18). "Like newborn infants, long for the pure spiritual milk, that by it you may grow up into salvation" (1 Peter 2:2).

Again I turn introspective, asking myself, *Am I growing in my knowledge of Christ?* Am I hungry for spiritual food that will nourish my stagnant soul? Or have I allowed my concept of Jesus to remain the same so that complacency has replaced expectation? If suddenly some magical unveiling of my level of spiritual maturity occurred, how would I appear to others? A toddler stumbling around in an ill-fitting adult suit?

I promise you, if we could gain a glimpse of Christ in the reality of his power, we would never yawn.

Unfortunately for Bob, and for many nominal Christians, Christ has remained peripheral, a child in a manger whom we reference at holidays, and perhaps in a repetitious prayer at mealtime. He certainly isn't in the place of reverence and centrality that he deserves.

Cute baby in the manger. Doesn't make any demands on my personal life. Doesn't say hard things about commitment and suffering. Smiles and coos and stays right where I put him, and doesn't complain when he's ignored all week long.

Things are about to get very tough for Bob and Sally. Let's hope their concept of Jesus can grow to meet their need.

2

ON PEDESTALS AND PLASTIC SMILES

Domesticating Jesus by Acting Christian

MEET SALLY. Sally Christian. Bob's wife. Mother of Bobby Jr. and Beth Ann. Life for Sally has been good, for the most part. She entered life with Bob with the excitement that they might have a real Christian family someday, but lately she's settled for a lot less. Bob's work is very demanding, pulling him toward the office with increasing hours that prevent family dinners together.

More pertinent to our story is Sally's Christian commitment. She came to Christ as a teen at a summer camp sponsored by Young Life. Unlike Bob, she made a real decision based on an understanding of her own sin and the ability of the cross to make everything all right again. Since that time, she has managed to grow a little in her faith, but lately her own work schedule and a pursuit of a master's in nursing has gotten in the way.

Was she concerned about marrying a non-Christian? Not at all. Because in Sally's mind Bob was a Christian. She was so excited after their first date. "You should have heard his prayer at dinner," she bubbled to her roommate. "He didn't just pray for the food. He took my hand and prayed for *us*."

Truthfully, Bob had learned that Christian girls let down their guard if they prayed together. He even managed to steal a wet kiss on his first date with Sally. Sadly, he was more excited about the effect of the prayer on Sally than on communication with the most awesome Creator of the universe.

Before I let you in on Bob and Sally's crisis, I want you to understand a problem that has plagued Sally since first becoming a Christian. She's not so unlike many of us. She wants everyone to like her. And because of that, she's been content to let others think of her in a positive light, even when it isn't true. Others have thought her spiritual, mature for her age as she came up through high school and university. It started simple enough. There was positive feedback for sharing a prayer request. Sometimes she found herself sharing a testimony where the emphasis shifted from glorifying Christ to an exaltation of her own spirituality. Of course, she quickly learned the lingo. "Praise the Lord" passed her lips almost as a space-filler instead of a heartfelt expression of honor to Christ.

As the months and years passed, Sally became something different in front of the saints of God than in her house alone. A plastic fakery crept in and dogged her until she was almost unaware at how much she'd changed. Without realizing it, a smile crept across her face when she entered the house of God. And not because she was happy to be among other Christians, but because the smile had become a habit, part of her makeup. *Let's see. I have lipstick, mascara, and my smile . . . all set!*

Had you asked, Sally wouldn't have acknowledged any vulnerability for an affair. But lately she'd grown weary of Bob's continual absence. His dedication to his work was taking its toll, especially on their relationship. And she was a committed wife, after all. If anything, she was jealous of Bob's secretary. He certainly spent more time with her than with Sally.

But today was destined to be a real test of their commitment.

How is Sally likely to react? Is her faith up to the test?

There are thousands of Christians like Sally. Truth be told, there's a little of Sally's experience in all of us. Perhaps it starts small. We are applauded or complimented for some spiritual insight or good deed. And down the road of men's approval we plod, anxious to keep up appearances. And the further down this road we travel, the more our faith loses its shine, and something less genuine takes its place.

People in leadership are particularly vulnerable to attack in this area. The idea creeps in that the congregation will lose faith in a leader who stumbles.

What they really want is a leader who is real.

It's not always the approval of men that prods us down the road toward fakery. Anytime we pass a period of genuine emotional infatuation with Christ and find ourselves in a dry spiritual desert, we may naturally fall into a religiosity that is more motion than substance. We will all face times like that. But times of dryness of soul, the times when the heavens seem closed, should prompt us to be sure that it isn't us that has moved away. If the season of dryness persists, we risk becoming a name-only Christian (if there really is something like that) or a congregation that gathers for the social interaction rather than to be fed by and to worship the King of Kings.

And that's what this book is all about in the down and dirty. We're small. God is big. Let's be real about our need and his supply. The world doesn't need a bunch of great Christians. It needs Christians who are real. Small people with a big God.

One of the largest stumbling blocks to Christianity is big Christians.

We domesticate Jesus when we act Christian. Not that we shouldn't behave in a Christian manner. But when we do, it shouldn't be an act. When we do that, we domesticate Christ.

How so?

Because any pretense that doesn't match reality fails to recognize where the attention is supposed to be—on his greatness. When we feel the need to be big in others' eyes, we've missed the whole point. What the world needs is an honest look at our smallness, and if anything of worth is accomplished by our hands, we point to Christ as the source. He gets the glory, and we get to climb down off the pedestal that we or others have built for us.

Missionaries face the pedestal temptation. So many Christians have a mental grading system for spirituality. It looks something like a bell curve with average Christians falling somewhere in the fat part of the curve, ministers falling a bit to the right, and missionaries at the very extreme. Must be spiritual, they think, because they're missionaries.

For people who put me up on a pedestal because I'm a missionary, I'm tempted to tell them a little story about my family. After all, missionary families must be special.

It was one of those brisk Kijabe Sunday mornings in Kenya, so all the windows were rolled up tight and we were in our car driving down from the local church. The boys were arguing about something. I don't remember what. It's not important now. But I do remember making it absolutely clear that no one was to get out of the car until each one of my sons had made peace with his brothers. Parents have different thresholds for tolerance of childhood rebellion, but I can assure you, willful, in-your-face disobedience tops the list of things parents just can't tolerate. Certainly the exalted missionary would have obedient children. So I pulled into our carport and said, "No one gets out until you're at peace with each other." Then Sam, my youngest, rather noisily spoiled the air and in less time than you could say "willful disobedience," everyone bailed out of the car.

What would my supporters think if I told them such a tale?

Hopefully, they would understand that we're just people, plain and simple. My only plea is God's grace, just like theirs.

We domesticate Christ when we think we are protecting his reputation to hide our weaknesses. This is a tragic mistake. What the world needs to see are Christians who are treasuring Christ for all that he is.

Paul calls us to relish our weaknesses. This is, of course, not a parading of our personal sin. What we want to parade is the cross and its provision. Speaking of the light of the gospel, Paul says,

> But we have this treasure in jars of clay, to show that the surpassing power belongs to God and not to us. (2 Corinthians 4:7)

> But he said to me, "My grace is sufficient for you, for my power is made perfect in weakness." Therefore I will boast all the more gladly of my weaknesses, so that the power of Christ may rest upon me. For the sake of Christ, then, I am content with weaknesses, insults, hardships, persecutions, and calamities. For when I am weak, then I am strong. (2 Corinthians 12:9–10)

This isn't mumbo-jumbo doublespeak. Paul is honestly and openly telling us that realization of our weaknesses prompts us to rely on strength outside of ourselves, the strength of the Almighty himself.

Subtly, for many Christians the self-made man syndrome has spilled into the church. Christianity is distorted into a celebration of my ministry, my service, and my worship. One false gospel of the domesticated Jesus centers around *me*. *My* testimony, *my* ability to do Christian stuff. It's all about *me*. Christ is cherished for what he does for me.

Now it's not wrong to cherish Christ for what he's done for us. But there is a subtle shifting of emphasis onto Christ serving me rather than me serving Christ.

In the next chapter I want to take our first look at just who Jesus really is. I believe it is in the context of our first glimpse of the real Jesus that we see our own selves in a healthy light. Exalting ourselves in the presence of the real Jesus makes no sense. We are babies flexing our muscles in front of Mr. Universe.

I want to begin to intersperse biblical images of Christ with our story of Bob and Sally Christian so we can have a parallel revelation of reality and their domesticated version.

A true knowledge of Christ, I believe, is critical and vital to our success as Christians. I can only imagine Satan and his minions being delighted at our acceptance of lesser Christs. *They want a Savior? I'll give them a savior. A nice, safe one who won't demand (or deserve) their awe and allegiance. One who is loving, yes, but not judgmental, and certainly not too demanding.*

My advice to Sally and myself is to get real. Avoid religious participation out of habit. As soon as we realize we've been placed on a pedestal, get off! To stay around only invites Christian fakery.

Above many other things, this book is a call to get real. Real with yourself. And real with God. It's time for me (and you) to take a serious look at who Jesus really is in the New Testament and to see if my life experience is matching up.

The further Christians plod down a pathway of pretending everything is OK in their Christian faith when they are not experiencing any heartfelt love for God or his unconditional grace, the harder it will get to see the real Jesus behind the domesticated model we've created.

I think it's interesting how Paul reacted to the public wanting to exalt him as a god. (And also amazing to see how fickle the people were to go from esteeming Paul as a god to stoning him . . . in only one verse!) He was in Lystra with Barnabas, and the crowd called Paul "Zeus," proclaiming that the god had taken on the form of a man. Paul decried his deity. We pick up the story in Acts 14, after Paul points them to the real God.

> Even with these words they scarcely restrained the people from offering sacrifice to them. But Jews came from Antioch and Iconium, and having persuaded the crowds, they stoned Paul and dragged him out of the city, supposing that he was dead. (vv. 18–19)

Wow. A pedestal is a dangerous place to be.

All I'm saying for now is that God is calling us into real relationship with him. He's not asking us to be spiritual or to act the part of someone we're not. When the chips are down and life gets tough, we're going to want to stand on something that's real.

And that's the beautiful thing about serving the real Jesus. He's strong enough, loving enough, graceful enough, and captivating enough to fulfill our longing and to outlive our boredom for eternity. This is the beginning, a call to be real and constantly cognizant of our need.

I'm small. But my flesh is constantly trying to cover that up and act big.

Conversely, the Jesus we serve is large. And yet our tendency throughout our Christian lives is to make him small enough to control. In essence, we've invited the Lord of the universe into the home of our lives and then asked him to sit in the corner and mind his own business. Sure, we give him an hour or two on Sundays, but we haven't given him access and free reign.

So who is he, and why is domesticating him such a tragedy?

Let's take a look and see.

3

THE BIGNESS OF THE REAL JESUS

Domesticating Jesus by
Underestimating His Power

I'M WRITING this chapter for those whose familiarity with Jesus begins and ends with holidays. Christmas and Easter. He's the baby in the manger or the man in the picture hanging on a cross, perhaps with a halo painted above his head. If you are a maturing Christian, this chapter is also for you. Because I know you are just like me. I need constant reminders of the reality of Jesus and his bigness.

We are living in a post-Christian era. No longer can it be assumed that growing up American means growing up Christian. As a missionary on foreign soil, I can tell you that the rest of the world, particularly the Muslim world, still views America as Christian. Oh how little they really know of our pagan society.

So I'm going to start with the basics. Jesus, the Son of God, is part of the Trinity. The Trinity is misunderstood by 1.5 billion of the world's citizens—Muslims who believe the Christian Trinity is Father, Jesus, and Mary. Wrong, but that's what they think.

Jesus did not originate on a cool night in Bethlehem. But essentially, most of his life before his brief period on earth is little understood and little revealed.

John enlightens us in his opening to his Gospel account.

In the beginning was the Word, and the Word was with God, and the Word was God. He was in the beginning with God. (John 1:1–2)

In the beginning?

Yes, as in Genesis 1:1: "In the beginning . . ."

Jesus was there from eternity past. What was he doing there? Keep reading.

All things were made through him, and without him was not any thing made that was made. (John 1:3)

Jesus was not only present at creation, but from these verses we know that he was involved in the creative process.

We know John was speaking of Jesus when he referred to the Word because he explains in verse 14:

And the Word became flesh and dwelt among us, and we have seen his glory, glory as of the only Son from the Father, full of grace and truth.

Yes, Jesus has been around since eternity past and has lived beyond the grave to live into future eternity.

I am the first and the last, and the living one. I died, and behold I am alive forevermore, and I have the keys of Death and Hades. (Revelation 1:17–18)

All it takes is a superficial understanding of the greatness of the universe to put me in a reflective mode. David says it like this:

When I look at your heavens, the work of your fingers,
   the moon and the stars, which you have set in place,
what is man that you are mindful of him,
   and the son of man that you care for him? (Psalm 8:3–4)

We know from powerful telescopes that there are billions of galaxies beyond our own, each with literally millions and millions of stars. The Perfect Spiral Galaxy was so named because it lies perpendicular to our own, and when viewed through a telescope, it forms a nearly perfect spiral. This galaxy is over thirty million light-years away. That's a number so large that I can't even begin to get my small brain around it. Light travels at 186,000 miles *each second*. In one year that amounts to a distance of 5.87 trillion miles, the distance of one light-year. Allow light to travel at 186,000 miles per second not just for one or two years or even a thousand years but *for over thirty million years* and finally it would reach the Perfect Spiral Galaxy.

Spend an hour on the Internet looking at other known galaxies. After only a few minutes the wow factor should be rocketing.

Now think.

This Jesus whom I serve formed this galaxy and billions others just with his word. Power like that is nearly incomprehensible.

This is the same Jesus who indwells our lives by his Spirit.

Behold, I stand at the door and knock. If anyone hears my voice and opens the door, I will come in to him and eat with him, and he with me. (Revelation 3:20)

To them God chose to make known how great among the Gentiles are the riches of the glory of this mystery, which is Christ in you, the hope of glory. (Colossians 1:27)

Could it be that I go about a significant part of my days ignoring a God so awesome?

Sadly, yes.

It is this God whom I wrap in the cloth of my small intellect and therefore ignore in a large part of my daily life.

The morning that Sally betrayed her husband and her own heart began like so many others: rushing to pack lunches for the kids, passing Bob in the hall on his way to the kitchen, without communication about the rest of their days. It was nothing special. Just another typical day in the fast lane.

She'd juggled life's demands successfully for so long, each ball being attended to for a short moment before it was launched into the air so she could catch the next ball before it crashed. The problem with too many balls is that you can't stop juggling without disaster.

In truth, her relationship with Bob had slid in recent months, but not alarmingly so. If you asked, she'd have explained it away as the normal waxing and waning of feelings that accompany a relationship stressed by business concerns and time constraints.

At work in the Memorial Hospital operating rooms, she was quickly absorbed into the color of trauma. A gunshot victim was bleeding out and would die without emergency surgery.

The anesthetic team established large-bore intravenous lines and squeezed in bags of dark blood. An assistant painted the abdomen with splashes of yellow Betadine.

She opened instruments, laying them out in order of suspected need.

Barry Stedman's eyes flashed above the glint of the scalpel. He made quick work of getting in and packing off the abdomen. Then, slowly removing the packs after anesthesia had finished playing catch-up, he discovered a shattered spleen. After five minutes of quick work, the damaged organ lay in a metal pan on the back sterile field. But the bleeding didn't stop. The liver had suffered a large stellate laceration.

Tension mounted. The clock slowed as Sally assisted the surgeon. Together they were able to bring a life back from the precipice of death. With gauze sponges packed tightly to tamponade the bleeding, the patient was moved to the ICU for further care.

Fresh with the exhilaration of their accomplishment, Sally withdrew with the surgeon into a private alcove just outside the operating room. They washed their hands at a common sink. To Sally, it seemed that she was washing away the tension.

She looked at Barry. "You were unbelievable. I thought we'd lost him."

He smiled, his eyes meeting hers. "I had great help."

Their eyes held as they pulled the surgical masks from their necks.

Barry had a small splatter of blood to the left of his eye. "Here," Sally said, reaching for his face with a cleansing sponge. She moved closer to him to wipe away the stain. She inspected the job, holding her position in front of him. Their breath mingled.

And then, with hearts pounding, their excitement over the patient-save dissolved in an embrace. Barry leaned forward, and Sally didn't back away.

Caution. Danger. Thrill. Warmth. Rising passion.

A few moments after Barry's hand found its way beneath Sally's scrub top, she pushed away. Breathless.

And guilty.

"I'm sorry," she whispered as she fled to the safety of the female changing room.

Late that afternoon, as Sally undressed at home after work, her mind seemed to spin from the memory of the moment she'd shared with Dr. Stedman. The seconds ticked from excitement to remorse to guilt and back to the tension of her attraction to the surgeon. She hung her blouse on the arm of her treadmill. That's when she noticed a small stain inside her brassiere. *Am I bleeding?*

She quickly confirmed her suspicions with a self-exam. *I can't feel anything. Could it just be some minor trauma from Barry?*

God must be punishing me.

It is not my intent to use these fictional illustrations to analyze the complexities of marriage or moral failure. I merely want to stimulate your thoughts into the common ways we so naturally limit Christ in our day-to-day lives. Now hopefully this experience hasn't struck too close to home, but if it has, there is certainly help for you too.

Notice how quickly Sally's mind becomes centered on guilt. If there's anything Christians are good at, it's this. We all feel guilty. I can hear your arguments already. Sally deserved to feel guilty!

I get that. But I also get that the gentle urgings of the Holy Spirit could be twisted and magnified in an unhealthy way.

I don't want to concentrate on her guilt just now. I'll devote most of a chapter to that later on. For now I want to reflect on her other reaction. Was God really punishing her?

No.

How do I know?

Because the cross of Calvary already took care of the punishment thing. Completely. Perfectly. All of our sins punished and covered. Past. Present. And future.

power. Words like great, awesome, marvelous, tremendous, and big are inadequate for him.

So I merely speak his name, realizing that in that one whispered name, all power, glory, and authority is expressed. And to make it personal, I simply refer to him as "you."

Sometimes as I walk up the rocky dirt road toward the hospital beneath the African sky, I whisper, "You," unable to say more. I'm not a particularly charismatic Christian, but somehow it feels right in that time to lift humble hands toward infinity.

In that moment, I'm dumbfounded. I stretch my hands toward the blackness of the night. "You, you."

This is the starting place to bringing home a reality glimpse of Jesus.

And that's all I'm able to give you.

A glimpse of greatness. Because the smallness of my brain will replace a great Jesus with a lesser option, one I have difficulty trusting with my everyday problems.

Meditate on the largeness of our Creator, the Christ who was the Word from the beginning of time. Start with the acknowledgment that we will never ever be able to get finite minds around the infinite. Our smallness can never really "get" his bigness. Remind your soul that the One who has taken residence up with us is too large to "get." That's a place I have to go to over and over and over again.

Get alone with God. And when words fail, as we only have human words and they are way, way too small, simply whisper the name that encompasses all power and greatness. And to make it personal, just say, "You."

4

A VERY BIG GOSPEL PLAN, PART 1

Domesticating Jesus by Wallowing in Guilt

FOR THE NEXT several weeks, Sally wore a plastic smile in front of a fearful heart. This was something, you remember, that she was particularly good at. Although she was a true Christian, she'd been playing to others' expectations for years, and so smiling was the Christian thing to do.

She saw the blood on three additional occasions, enough to convince her that it wasn't due to trauma. Now she worried about the "c" word.

She called her gynecologist who scheduled a mammogram and suggested a visit. She picked up her X-rays and brought them with her to the appointment. As she sat in her car outside her doctor's office, she read the radiologist's report. As she read, guilt played a discordant theme on the strings of her heart.

Her eyes scanned the mammogram report. "Cluster of micro-calcifications associated with irregular density retroareolar position, Right breast. Birads category 4. Biopsy recommended."

"God," she whispered, "why are you doing this to me?"

She sighed. Whether she believed it in her heart or not, she knew she couldn't successfully shove aside the accusations for long. *This is because you let Barry touch you. This is what you get for hiding the truth from your husband.*

She desperately wanted to pray for a miracle.

But she couldn't.

She didn't feel worthy.

She felt exactly one thing. Guilt. She'd gotten what she deserved.

Let's stop there for a minute. Poor Sally isn't so different than most of us. Even mature Christians think this way on occasion. It just seems natural to think that God will look approvingly on our prayers if we've been walking the straight and narrow.

But that's not the gospel of grace. That's the self-righteous false gospel that says, "Clean up so you'll be acceptable."

Which brings us to a second amazing teaching of Christianity: not only is Jesus the Creator of the universe, the one who created not just our galaxy but billions besides, he wants a relationship with people, his bride, the church. Because he's powerful and perfect, we need something to make us acceptable to God.

That something was the cross.

This cross was nothing less than the largest event of all history. This pivotal event was planned from the very beginning, even before creation. It is central to an understanding of the Christian gospel. Excuse me if you want to scan forward, yawning. *Yes, I know all about the cross.* But that's part of the problem with a domesticated Christ. We've made the cross small, in essence whittling it down to a decorative ornament that we can use as a Christian accessory. *Goes well with my Christian dress, don't you think?*

But this event is the biggest stumbling block to true faith. Many of us can look up to the heavens in amazement and imagine the bigness (imagine, I say, because I don't think we really grasp it) of the Creator. But when it comes down to believing that this huge and magnificent God actually wants a relationship with me, I hit the first hint of a bumpy road. *If he's so wonderful and awesome, what does he want with a relationship with me?*

Good question.

And we'll have to wait until heaven to get an adequate answer for it. But the truth remains. The Bible teaches us that this magnificent God loves us. *Loves* us. And so much that he planned our rescue from the origins of time,

> even as he chose us in him before the foundation of the world, that we should be holy and blameless before him. In love he predestined us for adoption as sons through Jesus Christ, according to the purpose of his will. (Ephesians 1:4–5)

> For God so loved the world, that he gave his only Son, that whoever believes in him should not perish but have eternal life. (John 3:16)

So many of us have heard this wonderful news, yet either don't believe it or give only a mental nod, not really getting our fingers around it and bringing it into our own experience.

In truth, if we believed it, truly *believed* it, we could never again for long entertain a guilty, undeserving thought. The truth of the gospel of grace assures our hearts that this incredible

Creator has unconditional love for us, that he lives *for* us. As we warm our hearts at the fireside of this truth, doubt, guilt, and fear are burned away.

Sadly, it is in the failure to grasp the concept of grace that we commonly domesticate our Lord. Instead of the loving Savior who died once for all of my sins past, present, and future, he becomes a God whom I can appease by my feeble attempts at good deeds.

While my good deeds might warm my heart and make me feel as if I've scored heavenly brownie points, it has added nothing to the cross. This is an essential truth of the gospel, that the cross has completely and perfectly paid for my sin debt and has resulted in the good deeds of Christ being exchanged for my pitiful efforts.

Because guilt is such a hang-up for so many Christians, I want to spend a bit more time on it here. As we dig deeper together to discover how we domesticate Jesus every day, I think we will see that it is common not to domesticate him with one huge mental move to dethrone him but in a thousand little worries, fears, and guilty feelings in which we've denied his power.

Domesticating Christ by Wallowing in Guilt

There's no other feeling like this one. Most of you know what I mean. It casts a threatening shadow across a sunshiny day. It robs us of joy. Destroys our effectiveness as believers. Zaps the happiness out of any blessing.

It's one of our enemy's favorite tools.

Think about it. One of our chief ends is to glorify God by seeing more and more people treasure God for who he really is. This is our great commission, to make disciples from every tribe, right? But when a Christian walks around with a cloud of guilt over his or her head, no one in his or her right mind would want to be like that. Ministry is effectively silenced. There's no more effective deterrent to becoming a believer than hanging around a miserable Christian.

So why do we do fall into it so easily?

Unbelief. We haven't let the forgiveness of Christ become real in our own experience.

Pride. If we're bent on control, we may think that we need to feel bad for a time so as to be worthy of forgiveness. This is junk, plain and simple. There is nothing that we can add to the cross of Christ to make ourselves more presentable to God. When he looks at a believer, he sees the righteousness of Christ.

We've listened to the whispers of our enemy. "You're not worthy. How can you call yourself a child of God when you _____?"

But doesn't the Holy Spirit convict us of sin?

Sure, but he doesn't condemn.

So how do we tell the difference?

Conviction focuses on restoration. Condemnation focuses on sin. Conviction is folded within the message of God's love and hope. Condemnation is folded within the message of hopelessness.

There was a time in my life when I needlessly felt guilty for any sin I felt had been directed toward another. I would continue to berate myself until I made a verbal confession. Only then would I let myself off the hook and experience the wonder of God's peace. But such heaviness was only detrimental to hearing God's voice. Too often I made a confession that was unnecessary. A minor infraction had been forgotten by the others involved. But my guilt drove me forward, and I couldn't hear the gentle whispers of God's Spirit.

We need to realize that our guilt has been dealt with on the cross for sins past, present, and future. We may need to make a confession in order to restore fellowship with God or another, but the issue of guilt has been settled long before confession is made.

To continue to punish ourselves for sins for which Jesus died is an insult in the face of a most gracious and merciful Father.

Do you feel it is appropriate to spend a little time in misery so as to show proper penance? Do you think you deserve to feel bad for your sins?

Perhaps so, but walking around punishing yourself for old sins is a case of gospel debt, pure and simple. There is nothing more we can do to make ourselves more acceptable than that which has already been done on the cross. Any amount of squirming about in self-flagellation is worse than futile; it's arrogant.

Arrogant? Yes. How do we dare think that the work that Christ has performed has not been adequate? When we wallow in guilt, we act as if we are adding to a job that Jesus describes as, "Been there, done that."

Dear brother or sister, spend your time at the foot of the cross in amazement at the sacrifice he made. Look no longer to your sin but toward the One who became sin for us. Turn away from your guilt, and waste no further time in this grievous activity.

This is one of those conditions that may require some dedicated time in God's presence, soaking in the reality of what has been done for you. I've known times when I felt that the fight against the guilt emotion was hopeless. My brain acknowledged the truth of forgiveness, but it seemed my soul was trapped in a web of remorse over my sin. But I believe that with time we can train our minds to think according to biblical truth, and as we do, proper feelings will follow. In that way, feelings cannot be the focus of our intervention, but they often prompt a closer look at what may be driving the problem.

It becomes a matter of the will. We make a conscious decision to direct our thinking according to truth presented in the gospel. Christ died in my place. My sin has been covered. Christ's record is now mine.

Where Is My Focus?

It is a practical truth that we become like what we behold. If your children are constantly admiring a certain Hollywood favorite, you may soon be amused (or disgusted!) at the language and mannerisms of the person they admire because they will be one and the same as the language and gestures of your children.

It is also a biblical principle that as we spend time in God's presence, we are changed. "And we all, with unveiled face, beholding the glory of the Lord, are being transformed into the same image from one degree of glory to another. For this comes from the Lord who is the Spirit" (2 Corinthians 3:18).

Focus on myself, and I'll be tempted toward despair. My weaknesses, sin, and problems loom large as they become the center of my thoughts. Take anything small—say your thumb—and pull it close enough to your eyes, and it will eventually block out the vision of anything. In a position just in front of your face, your thumb can block out the Empire State Building.

You see, perspective is everything. What our souls need is the perspective of the gospel of grace.

Behold the glory of the Lord and be changed, "from one degree of glory to another." Stare at myself and I'll be changed from one degree of discouragement to another. A sure recipe for a miserable day.

My point? Simply that we need to consciously direct our thoughts onto Christ and what he has done for us, settling for eternity the outcome of our salvation. With every thought of condemnation, we need to mentally shift gears onto the fact that we have been forgiven. If this is practiced over and over, we can construct a new path for our thoughts to follow. In time we will automatically use a condemning thought to prompt amazement at our great salvation.

We are instructed to lay aside every sin that so easily entangles us. That includes every aspect of the sin right down to the condemnation it precipitates.

> Therefore, since we are surrounded by so great a cloud of witnesses, let us also lay aside every weight, and sin which clings so closely, and let us run with endurance the race that is set before us, looking to Jesus, the founder and perfecter of our faith, who for the joy that was set before him endured the cross, despising the shame, and is seated at the right hand of the throne of God. Consider him who endured from sinners such hostility against himself, so that you may not grow weary or fainthearted. (Hebrews 12:1–3)

Notice the instruction. How do we lay aside every weight (guilt) and sin? Look to Jesus, not to our sin. Consider him, not ourselves.

In Philippians 4, Paul gives us specific instructions regarding our thought life. If we want relief from a guilty conscience, we need to focus our thoughts on the positive items listed in verse 8:

> Finally, brothers, whatever is true, whatever is honorable, whatever is just, whatever is pure, whatever is lovely, what-

ever is commendable, if there is any excellence, if there is anything worthy of praise, think about these things. What you have learned and received and heard and seen in me—practice these things, and the God of peace will be with you. (Philippians 4:8–9)

Is your sin honorable, pure, lovely, commendable, excellent, or worthy of praise?

Of course not. Then, according to the apostle Paul, we are not to dwell on it.

We are to put on the helmet of salvation. We are in a war, and the battleground is our mind, will, and emotions.

Controlling the thought life is a real part of the battle, and proper feelings follow proper thoughts like a caboose follows the engine.

For the weapons of our warfare are not of the flesh but have divine power to destroy strongholds. We destroy arguments and every lofty opinion raised against the knowledge of God, and take every thought captive to obey Christ, being ready to punish every disobedience, when your obedience is complete. (2 Corinthians 10:4–6)

Every thought captive. Wow. This is more than just training ourselves to think positively. It is holding the truth of the gospel in constant focus before our eyes, so that its truth can wash us over and over and over.

To set the mind on the flesh is death, but to set the mind on the Spirit is life and peace. (Romans 8:6)

I love the way this reads in *The Message*, the contemporary language paraphrase by Eugene Peterson:

Obsession with self in these matters is a dead end; attention to God leads us out into the open, into a spacious, free life.

Want a day where every footstep is mired by guilt that clings like mud on your soul? Just spend a day thinking about your own sin.

Conversely, spend a day with your mind focused on the work of Christ, and peace is the outcome.

> You keep him in perfect peace
>   whose mind is stayed on you,
>   because he trusts in you. (Isaiah 26:3)

I want to mention another principle here. Abiding Christian fruit such as the peace of God that overcomes our guilt comes as a result of sinking our roots deep into Christ. Most of us are familiar with John 15. Abiding in the vine is the only way to bear fruit.

> He is like a tree
>   planted by streams of water
> that yields its fruit in its season,
>   and its leaf does not wither.
> In all that he does, he prospers. (Psalm 1:3)

To whom is the verse referring? How can we experience enduring fruit (including relief of guilt) like this? Back up one verse.

> But his delight is in the law of the Lord,
>   and on his law he meditates day and night. (Psalm 1:2)

Let's go over the priorities once more to lay this problem to rest.

Can't stop feeling guilty?

Can you see that laboring beneath a load of guilt is a symptom that you have slipped away from the truth of the gospel? Or has your pride, the sense that you need to punish yourself (in essence taking God's role) kept you from acknowledging your need? If you realize that wallowing in guilt is a symptom of your reliance on a false gospel, you've opened the way to proceed to believing the gospel promises. Communion with these promises is the essence of the third step. Meditate on these promises every time you find yourself stumbling into the guilt trap.

There is therefore now no condemnation for those who are in Christ Jesus. (Romans 8:1)

Therefore, since we have been justified by faith, we have peace with God through our Lord Jesus Christ. (Romans 5:1)

For God did not send his Son into the world to condemn the world, but in order that the world might be saved through him. (John 3:17)

If we confess our sins, he is faithful and just to forgive us our sins and to cleanse us from all unrighteousness. (1 John 1:9)

For freedom Christ has set us free; stand firm therefore, and do not submit again to a yoke of slavery. (Galatians 5:1)

Let us then with confidence draw near to the throne of grace, that we may receive mercy and find grace to help in time of need. (Hebrews 4:16)

But when Christ had offered for all time a single sacrifice for sins, he sat down at the right hand of God, waiting from that time until his enemies should be made a footstool for his feet.

For by a single offering he has perfected for all time those who are being sanctified. (Hebrews 10:12–14)

Who shall bring any charge against God's elect? It is God who justifies. Who is to condemn? Christ Jesus is the one who died—more than that, who was raised—who is at the right hand of God, who indeed is interceding for us. (Romans 8:33–34)

By this we shall know that we are of the truth and reassure our heart before him; for whenever our heart condemns us, God is greater than our heart, and he knows everything. (1 John 3:19–20)

Not only does the true gospel solve the sin dilemma, it takes care of the guilt and provides the salve to soothe our soul-hurt. We fall into domesticating Jesus when we belittle his salvation plan or the cross on which he died.

Jesus is huge. His plan of salvation is 100 percent effective. The cross is all that is needed to set me before my Heavenly Father in a perfect state. To add anything to the cross is domestication.

5

AN UNPREDICTABLE, MIRACULOUS JESUS

Domesticating Jesus in a Safe, Scientific Box

THAT NIGHT, Sally waited until the children had left the dinner table to bring up the news from her doctor's visit. "I went to see Dr. Myers today."

Bob looked up from his second helping of lasagna.

"There is an abnormality on my mammogram. He's set me up for a biopsy."

Her husband set down his fork and leaned forward. "W-what'd he say? Lots of women get biopsies, right?" He cleared his throat. "It could be nothing, right?"

She nodded, not wanting her voice to crack.

Bob reached for her hand. "Sally?"

"I just keep thinking about my mom."

He shook his head. "Let's not go there. You are nothing like your mom. She had a lump in her breast for a year before she even told your dad."

She sniffed. "He said the mammogram is very worrisome."

"When is the biopsy?"

"Tuesday."

Bob's face sobered. "Not wasting any time, are they?" He stood up and pulled the phone book out of a kitchen cabinet.

"What are you doing?"

"I want to call Pastor Wally."

"No," she said, a bit more forcefully than she'd intended. "Let's not bother him."

"Sally, that's what he's there for. I want to ask him to pray."

"We don't even have a diagnosis, Bob. I don't want you to tell him." She hesitated. "Not yet."

She turned away, her thoughts unspoken. Sally felt unworthy to ask for prayer.

"Let's ask God to do a miracle."

"Since when do you talk like that? You always make fun of those healin' preacher-types."

"I'm not talking about going to some healer. I just think we should ask God, that's all."

Sally walked to the kitchen sink and looked out the window into the backyard. She knew Bob meant well, but she didn't feel like praying. How could she pray when she felt like she'd brought all of this on herself? She'd been flirting with Barry for weeks. Finally he kissed her. Then her bleeding started. Even if it was just a coincidence, the timing made her feel so guilty. Finally she turned around. "Have you actually ever known God to do a miracle?"

Bob shook his head.

"Don't be naïve, Bob. God has given us doctors to know what to do in these situations." She paused. "I think I'll stick to what I know to be right."

For a number of reasons, our western society has become skeptical of the supernatural. We say we believe God can do miracles, but in our hearts we doubt he'll ever do one on our behalf. So, like Sally (but maybe for different reasons), we've moved away from anything we deem flaky and prefer to rely on science and the laws of nature.

Of course, if I thought people should only pray and not go to their doctors, I wouldn't be true to myself or my readers. I'm a surgeon. I've spent the majority of my life preparing for or performing surgery to aid physical healing.

But too often we may launch a prayer for a miracle to the sky, but the Jesus we've created is much too small to actually get out of his box and do a miracle. We have plenty of reasons why he won't.

"We have the Bible now. We don't need miracles to convince us to believe."

"That's what faith is for, right? We believe even though we haven't seen."

"God has given us intelligence, medical science, and doctors. That's miracle enough."

For some reason, God seems to hold back from behaving in ways we deem miraculous. But that doesn't mean he can't or won't. That's my point. Not believing that he could step out of the "norm" and do a miracle is nothing short of domesticating him again.

As a surgeon I have come face-to-face with my own bias against the supernatural, miraculous workings of God. I'm used to God operating in a predictable and definable way. In other words, he normally uses medicine and surgery to accomplish healings. Sure, I pray for healing, I pray with patients, but sometimes I realize I'm not expecting God to step out of the box I've mentally prepared for him.

It's been six or seven years since I saw my first out-of-the-box-God miracle. I saw a young lady in my office (then in her upper twenties). She had a hard, irregular mass in her left breast and a mammogram that was very suspicious for cancer. I aspirated some cells using a needle and syringe and sent them to a pathologist who confirmed the diagnosis of cancer.

I saw my patient back in the office and talked over her options. She decided to have a removal of the lump and the lymph nodes under her arm with plans to follow up with radiotherapy. One evening a few days later, after I'd scheduled my patient for surgery, I got a call from her.

"I don't need that surgery. I went to my pastor. He prayed for me, and I've been healed."

I confess that my first reaction was anything but filled with faith. Skepticism, yes. Faith, no.

I rolled my eyes. "Can you come into the office and show me?"

She agreed.

I fully anticipated showing her the mass to help overcome her "denial."

A few days later, I stood over her, examining her as I'd done on the first visit. *That's strange*, I thought. *I don't feel anything abnormal.* I consulted the patient record, reading again my description and reminding myself of the location. I returned to examine her a second time. At that point I opened my mouth but couldn't bring myself to acknowledge a miracle. "I don't know what has happened to you," I said. (If that isn't a statement lacking faith, I don't know what is!)

I ordered another mammogram. The radiologist called, not wanting to repeat an unnecessary X-ray on such a young patient. "Just do it," I urged. "Things have changed, and I need to see a new mammogram."

The radiologist resisted but finally relented after my urging.

The new mammogram looked nothing like the first. Gone was the angry mass. In its place a vague shadow remained.

In the absence of any palpable abnormality in the breast, I asked that the patient let me do a biopsy guided by a mammographically-placed wire. I planned to follow the wire down to the concerning shadow and remove it.

She and her husband were very reluctant to undergo an unnecessary procedure. I urged strongly, using the example of the lepers whom Jesus healed as examples. "Jesus told them to show themselves to the priest to confirm their healing. I need you to let me show this tissue to the pathologist to confirm what is going on."

She relented. I did the biopsy, and guess what? No cancer! When I gave the results to the patient and her husband, his response was predictable. "I told ya so, Doc."

But professional people began to wonder. Maybe the pathologist who read the original needle test was wrong.

So I sent the pathology slides to the University of Virginia and had their pathologists review it. They confirmed the first pathologist's findings. This was cancer, pure and simple.

I've followed that patient for over five years, and she has remained cancer-free, never even having a mammographic suspicion of cancer.

I know Jesus can heal in this way. So how can I justify my first response when my patient suggested that Jesus had healed her?

Could it be that I'd domesticated him into a safe, predictable box?

59

There are some things that foreign missionaries are reluctant to share with their home churches. One might be the miraculous, unpredictable way that God behaves.

I've heard some of their stories. It's the kind of thing that comes out late at night, when missionaries are conferencing together, long after the last session has ended.

A number of years ago, some Africa Inland Missionaries met with the unexpected on the shores of Lake Victoria. It seemed that on one of the islands, the children had fallen under a curse of a local witchdoctor. The children from a primitive village were running into the lake in an attempt to drown themselves.

That's when concerned parents sought the help of some of my fellow AIM missionaries. "Come and help our children," they pleaded.

So missionary Dale Hamilton followed the villagers to the small island. And there on the sandy shore in the middle of Lake Victoria, he encountered the unexpected.

Uneducated children, who knew only their own tribal language, spoke to Dale in clear English. He understood immediately. The man-sized, guttural voice coming through the children was demonic.

A young girl physically attacked him, demonstrating supernatural strength. This was a spiritual war, up close and personal. Dale fended off his attacker and began renouncing and rebuking the forces of darkness in the name of Jesus.

And you'd better believe that the name he invoked was not the name of an inferior, domesticated version.

It was the name above all names. The name of an all-powerful and all-knowing God, ruler of all that is seen *and unseen*.

Why are foreign missionaries reluctant to share some of these very real spiritual encounters with their supporters back home?

Because so many of those supporters would find the stories incredible to the point of disbelief. They are so used to the spirit world (including Jesus) behaving in a certain way that they have trouble believing when Jesus chooses to "step outside the box" and behave in a supernatural way.

Missionaries understand the bias of their sending churches. They fear a withdrawal of needed support from fellow Christians who think that, in light of the spectacular stories, the missionary must have fallen off the deep end!

We seem most comfortable with Jesus' human side. But remember, he is also God. His power is unlimited. He can heal with the assistance of doctors and medicine, or he can heal miraculously.

He can obey the laws of nature (he usually does, as he's the one who set them in motion) or, he can completely defy them.

Remember the WWJD bracelets? They were reminders that we are to live our lives in awareness of how Jesus would behave in certain situations. "What would Jesus do?" was to be the guiding question.

But as I read the Gospel accounts of Jesus' actions, sometimes I find his next words and actions hard to predict. So often Jesus cast off the roles that were being forced upon him and behaved in unpredictable ways.

An easier question for me to answer is this: What would a domesticated Jesus do?

Whatever I predict, that's what. Because I have him in a box and allow him to act only in pre-approved ways.

Sometimes I need to remind myself that Jesus is supernatural. I need to remember he is limited *only in my mind.*

6

A VERY BIG GOSPEL PLAN,
PART 2

*Domesticating Jesus by Underestimating
the Power of the Gospel*

WE'VE SPENT TIME looking at the bigness of Christ,
the fact that he is the Creator of the universe and the fact that,
at times, he does step out of the box and reveal himself in totally
miraculous ways. That's his prerogative. After all, he's God.

But the truth of the matter is that it seems that Jesus doesn't
reveal himself to us in his power or glory very often. In fact, no
one has ever experienced the full extent of his greatness. We're
just not made to withstand that kind of glory.

So I've settled into a life similar to that of many Christians
where my expectations of the "supernatural" are limited, and I
anticipate God's following "the rules." And yet my tendency to
domesticate him falls into a more constant, mundane pattern.

I'm using the term *domesticate* here in a broader sense. Domesticating Christ is more than just formulating him in my mind as a servant to my will and wants, the ultimate vending-machine-in-the-sky phenomenon. I domesticate Jesus when I do anything that underestimates his ability. It is in the small things where I see the most problems in my own life. Perhaps you can relate.

Have you ever been tempted to think, *What good is it to be a Christian? I have the same problems as everyone else.*

You're not alone. I've been there too. It's all a part of our tendency to make small the Lord of the Universe.

If you struggle with insecurity, anxiety, lust, bitterness, or anger, you may just be human after all. Being human means we possess a tendency to formulate God within limited human concepts and framework.

If you've struggled to see the relevancy of Christ to your work, your play, or your everyday life, then read on, tired comrade, 'cause I've been there as well.

In Hebrews 7:25 we read, "Consequently, he is able to save to the uttermost those who draw near to God through him, since he always lives to make intercession for them."

Yet these words don't jive with our experience. We attend church on Sunday, but we struggle to see the relevance of faith to our minute-by-minute battles. We look at those in the pews beside us, and what do we see? All too often we find people with deep emotional hurts, anger, and anxiety. What does being saved "to the uttermost" mean for them? For me?

Does it mean that the gospel changes everything, that its truth should penetrate and redeem every part of my life, 24/7?

Exactly.

The gospel impacts the way I think, the way I act, the way I view myself and the world around me. In short, by the gospel of grace I'm a new creation. The gospel plan of salvation is *huge*. Just like Jesus.

"To the uttermost" means the gospel changes me spiritually, emotionally, socially, even physically.

Anyone who has attended church services is familiar with the Sunday-Monday disconnect. We give God an hour on Sunday morning and then resume lives that are indistinguishable from everyone else's. In that respect, it's more of a Sunday noon to Sunday one o'clock disconnect. It's a result of the western idea that compartmentalizes rather than integrates the different areas of our lives.

But the gospel should impact my work, play, social, and family interactions and my "religious life."

Too many of us see Christianity as a fire escape. We've heard the message of salvation, and we readily asked Jesus into our hearts (a phrase, by the way, that expresses a sincere idea but doesn't really convey a rounded, biblical concept of salvation), but we've walked away unchanged.

It's no less crazy than a nuclear explosion without fallout. Let's be honest. Salvation without evidence isn't real.

But all Christians struggle. Real Christians. We all have our anxious moments, our moments of anger. We struggle with bitterness and lust. Does that mean we're not "in"? Of course not.

But it does mean we're not experiencing salvation to the uttermost at that moment. To borrow a phrase from the apostle Paul, we've fallen from grace. And to continue with our theme, we can see that experiencing less than salvation to the uttermost is a type of domestication of Christ.

So what can we do when we find ourselves in the throes of these common, everyday struggles? Can my knowledge of the gospel of grace really impact my thinking concerning my relationship with my neighbor, my boss, my spouse, or my children?

Does the Christian gospel have an application where the rubber meets the road? Can it influence a life of discouragement, worry, self-condemnation, lust, and defeat?

Of course. Domestication of Christ is so much more than failure to expect him to work in a miraculous way or the failure to think of him as the One capable of breathing out stars.

Is the gospel as weak as we make it appear to the world, a philosophy without the power to make a difference that sets us apart the way we were intended to be? God forbid!

One of my first encounters with the fact that the gospel was truth to be taken seriously in all of life came when I was a senior in high school. I'd been talking with a local pastor, a godly man who'd given up a career in engineering to serve in the pulpit. We were discussing a certain matter when he suggested we pray for guidance. After the "amen" was spoken, he lifted his head and asked, "So what do you sense God saying to you?"

I was taken aback. I'd been brought up as a Christian and had participated in prayers like that one hundreds of times, but this man actually believed that God was going to lead us as we requested. On the spot, I must have mumbled something. I walked away from that meeting with a new appreciation for the pastor's simple faith. Since then I've met hundreds, perhaps thousands, of Christians who talk the talk but never walk the walk. They call themselves Christians but never actually believe the gospel is true for them. Maybe they give it mental assent, but it never sinks beneath the dermis.

Has church attendance become a necessary additive to achieve social status? Are we walking through the motions but not experiencing the amazing benefits of sonship?

The Christian faith was never intended to be an outward whitewash. The gospel is not meant to be merely life-altering. It's all about *a completely new life*. A life characterized by love at its center. Just as our DNA encodes every characteristic of our physical life, so there are certain characteristics that are intended to define the Christian: love, peace, joyfulness, faithfulness, gentleness, and generosity, for example.

So what about all of the times when life's disasters challenge us and defeat us, and as a consequence our lives look nothing like the life of contentment, joy, and love that God intended?

How can we move from domesticating Christ through our smallness to experiencing his largeness in the contented, joy-filled life that he intended?

I've spent my career as a surgeon handling patients in physical crises. And almost invariably when a patient is in crisis, numerous distractions tempt the physician to turn away from the critical issues at hand. Take a trauma patient, the victim of a motor vehicle accident, for example. The patient's leg is bent at a sickening angle. The patient is screaming. Maybe drunk. There's blood on his clothing. A student nurse is asking questions. A family member is crying, "Do something!" The intercom is sounding a call for a physician to dial a certain number. The patient vomits on your shoes.

It's all part of the milieu of distraction that a surgeon learns to push into the background like so much of the noise of life so that the critical needs can be assessed and appropriate action initiated.

A is for airway. **B** is for breathing. **C** is for circulation. I've done it so many times that it has become reflex.

The underlying problem with the patient with critically low blood pressure is something known as *oxygen debt*, a lack of sufficient oxygen getting to the cells. Without it, cells die, and the metabolic machinery unravels in a spiral toward death. It's vital stuff of the life-and-death variety. That's why the simplicity of the ABCs is of paramount importance. Death will occur within minutes without adequate oxygen.

I've come to see that so many of the daily crises that come my way are results of my failure to walk in the provisions set forth by the gospel of grace. Perhaps it's anxiety or discouragement. If you dissect beneath the surface, you'll come to see that I've slipped away from grace. And remember, small problems, ignored or accepted as part of the normative experience, can compound and grow. Eventually our spiritual life is gasping.

You may be tempted to think, *Come on, you're not saying that the gospel of grace can impact the way I deal with routine everyday, run-of-the-mill struggles, are you?*

Sure. Take anxiety for example.

The gospel is about salvation. What does that have to do with worry? You see, if I take a spiritual scalpel to my life, I'll quickly expose my anxiety for what it really is: I've started relying on a false gospel of pride instead of on my loving Father. The gospel is so much bigger than just a get-out-of-hell-free card. The gospel is this: Jesus Christ died on the cross to accomplish the great exchange. My sin-debt is paid, and Christ's righteousness is added to my account, placing me in right standing before a perfect God. As a result of this event, I am a new creation, a happening akin to a spiritual nuclear explosion. The resulting fallout from the gospel is huge and lifelong. I'm a son of the Lord of all creation and am entitled to walk forward through life without relying on my own ability to stand perfect and accepted before God. It's all a matter of grace.

Gospel Debt: When My Soul Is Demanding Payment and the Currency Is Grace

When I'm in the doldrums of reliance on a false gospel, I've fallen into a situation that I call *gospel debt*—my soul is demanding payment and the currency is grace, which I am at that time refusing. Like oxygen debt, a situation that can be fatal and needs urgent attention, gospel debt is no less critical to my spiritual well-being. The problem is, we've come to accept many symptoms of gospel debt as the normal experience. We've resigned ourselves to lives of defeat, bitterness, worry, and loneliness. We've made Jesus small in our minds, a God incapable of being trusted with our current misery.

The everyday experience of most Christians looks nothing like the completely grace-saturated, joyous life that Jesus knew.

But it doesn't have to be that way. What we've done, in effect, is just what the author of the book of Hebrews was talking about when he said, "how shall we escape if we neglect such a great salvation?" (2:3). This great salvation, this great gospel, means that we can live lives of love, joy, and peace in abundance. We can have lives that are free of the entanglements of greed, bitterness, and unforgiveness. We can live free of anxiety and anger.

But how?

Most Christians I know are just as miserable as anyone else. And many are worse, because they feel guilty for falling so short of their own expectations. They sin and can't even enjoy it because of the self-condemnation.

Sadly true. But true only because they are living lives in gospel debt, unaware of the nuclear fallout that should be part and parcel of the Christian experience.

So that's what this book is going to focus on: moving practically from Hebrews 2:3 to Hebrews 7:25. Going from neglect of a great salvation to being saved to the uttermost. From the domestication of Christ to recognition that he is big enough to handle our current situation.

Do you long for a life free of ball-and-chain obsessions with guilt? We looked in the last chapter at domesticating Christ by wallowing in guilt.

Have you given up hope on beating a sin that ensnares you over and over?

Do you thirst for communion with your loving Father, a life of constant grace-awareness rather than self-awareness? Haven't we had enough of that?

If the gospel really provides for the abundant life that Jesus promised us in John 10:10 ("I came that they may have life and have it abundantly"), then why is it such a rarity in Christian circles?

Have you ever been tempted to run with nonbelievers because Christians are such a drag? Have you ever thought that you might as well live like a non-Christian because at least that way you could enjoy sinning for a change?

It's because we have it all wrong!

We've neglected our great salvation. We've fallen from grace. We're in gospel debt without a clue as to how we got there or how to go about getting help. Alas, we've made a big God small.

The abundant life is such a rarity among Christians because we're paying attention to all of the distractions, the background noise that keeps our focus away from the critical needs. We need a spiritual resuscitation to assist our souls out of gospel debt and into grace saturation, a state where we recognize that we've been *saved to the uttermost.*

This book is practical by design. I want to assist you in your struggle with life's small daily disasters. Worry. Anger. Bitterness. Habitual sins. These are life's daily problems, the ones that creep up over and over and rob us of peace and contentment. By intention I've decided to focus on the little irritations in life that leave our souls in a chronic state of dryness.

I've chosen to use the term *domestication* to frame the times when we've slipped from the life God intended us to have because I hope that it will shock us into an honest look at how ridiculous it is to worry when we are being held by the One who created *everything*. Think of it as a spiritual defibrillation of sorts. Certainly you've seen it a dozen times on TV. A patient's heart has failed, and the doctor brings out the paddles to shock the patient back into a stable rhythm. *All clear!*

That's what this book is about. Shocking you (and me) into right thinking about the bigness of God and his ability to handle the things that are dragging us down.

So how do we move from domesticating Christ, a situation that we fall into almost as easily as breathing, into the full life God intended, a life where the bigness of Jesus is recognized and celebrated?

Let's go back to our oxygen metaphor.

Oxygen debt is a normal part of life. We run up a hill, and our muscles begin to cry out, "Send more oxygen!"

As a result, a series of compensating events occur. Our respiratory rate increases. Our hearts beat faster, and soon the currency of oxygen is delivered and the debt is paid. If we're out of shape, oxygen debt comes more quickly and with less exertion, and we recover more slowly. If we're in top physical form, oxygen debt becomes a rare experience, and our recovery from oxygen debt is quicker.

Similarly, gospel debt is a normal part of the Christian experience. We all fail to keep the cross of Christ in focus, and as a consequence we fall prey to a myriad of frail attempts to make up for a perceived lack of acceptance before our Father. We fall from the gospel of grace and attempt to make ourselves more acceptable by working harder, and we feel guilty and anxious in the process.

But if we're in top spiritual form, our lapses into gospel debt become rare, and our recovery quicker.

71

That's where this challenge comes in. It's a handy reminder of the resuscitation that will make our time spent in gospel debt a rarity and assists our recovery.

We can't stop life's daily disasters.

But we can learn to respond in a way that reflects the truth of the gospel and the bigness of our God.

In a life lived in constant grace appreciation, peace replaces anxiety, hope dislodges fear, forgiveness trumps resentment, generosity wins over greed, and joy rises over sorrow. In a life where the bigness of Jesus is celebrated, our problems look small in comparison. Conversely, in a life where Christ is domesticated, our problems take center stage.

How can we find such a life of peace, joy, forgiveness, and generosity?

It starts with God. We focus on the bigness of Jesus and his provision through a very big gospel plan for our rescue, a plan that moves way beyond our deliverance from hellfire.

A Note of Caution

This life is available to all believers.

But few have the discipline to find it. The distractions are too great and our view of the true gospel and Jesus too small.

I feel the need for a final note of caution before we launch ahead, looking at practical solutions. This book isn't a guarantee for an easy life. That would be presumptuous folly. When we take the hand of Christ in relationship, not only are we holding the hand of the Creator of the universe, we're holding a hand scarred by nails. When we agree to follow him, he demands a life of sacrifice and promises suffering along the way.

Yet this is the path to the abundance he promises.

Abundance of sustaining grace, not necessarily an absence of pain.

Abundance of joy, regardless of circumstances.

Abundance of contentment, regardless of our financial state.

Abundance of peace even when we deserve guilt.

Our lives can be defined by his love the way he intended, instead of ruled by events beyond our control.

It's the life Christians dream for . . . and a life that is ours by birthright.

This book is practical, a guide to help keep us on the path. It is repetitive by design, because I seem to be wired to forget how much he loves me and to lean on my own abilities. Just because we recognize the bigness of Jesus doesn't imply that this is a quick process to obtain Christian victory or perfection. This is simply another memory jog that I need, a mental shocker if you will, that I need over and over as I find myself waylaid by life.

And hopefully, someday, the process will approach reflex. I won't be pulled aside by all the distractions. I'll focus on the crisis at hand and recognize it for the gospel debt it is, recognize my tendency to domesticate Christ, and start back on the road to spiritual balance again.

In each chapter you'll find Scripture so that you can quickly find the references you need, the promises that God makes to us as his children. It's the provision of the gospel of grace. I won't apologize for quoting an abundance of verses. If anything can nudge your soul back into grace saturation (and out of Christ-domestication), it's meditating on the words of God, and I wanted to include them here so this can be a handy reference for key promises.

Let's get to it. Along the way, we'll look in on Bob and Sally to see what we can learn from their struggles.

7

"BUT WHATIF?"

Domesticating Jesus by Our Worry

BACK TO SALLY. Biopsy day came and went with one major complication: Bob missed it entirely. Because of an emergency meeting with a business client, Bob had headed to St. Louis. Oh, he had his wife's verbal blessing. "Go," she said, "there's nothing that we're going to know tomorrow anyway. You can go with me to get the results of the biopsy when it's available."

But husbands should realize that what wives say with their lips doesn't always correlate with the desires in their hearts. This was one of those times, and Bob blew it big-time. He should have insisted that he be at Sally's side.

A second complication could have been viewed as major: Barry Stedman sent flowers. Meanwhile, Bob sent a text message on his phone, letting her know that his business deal had proceeded without a hitch.

When Bob came home late that night, Sally had entered a world of worry that even her normal plastic smile couldn't hide.

Cancer. I know it's cancer. What will Bobby Jr. and Beth Ann do without me? What will happen to my marriage? Should I tell Bob what happened between Barry and me? How will we afford our mortgage if I have to quit work?

Bob looked at the bouquet of flowers on the kitchen table. He lifted a leaf and grunted.

Sally could see a stab of concern on her husband's face. He knew he'd blown it. He hadn't sent flowers. "They're from the folks at work," she said, white-lying her way away from the truth.

"How do you feel?"

"Worried."

Bob wrapped his arms around her and sighed. "Me too, baby. Me too."

Do you have an overactive "what-ifer"?

A what?

You know, something in your brain that can't seem to quit going over possible negative outcomes for your circumstances. If you're like so many others, you probably just downplay it.

"I'm just a worrier."

"I've always been high-strung."

"I'm just attentive to details."

My wife and I have a playful way to remind each other that we've slipped into needless worry. There is a delightful family Christmas TV special that we saw a number of years ago. It is called *The Best Christmas Pageant Ever*, and is the story of a church congregation putting on a Christmas play. As the practices go on, one little boy continually asks the director of the play, "But whatif I get thick?"

I write it that way because he says "what if" as if it is one word, "whatif," and because he has a lisp, he says "thick" for "sick." Over and over he asks, "But whatif I get thick?"

When Kris catches me worrying, she imitates the little boy's voice and says, "But whatif?" It's her gentle reminder that I'm spinning off into gospel debt. To put it in context with our present discussion, think about how crazy it is to worry when my hand is held by the One who made the stars. When I worry, I've made Jesus small again. Too small to handle my problems. It's one of the most common ways that Christians domesticate Christ every day.

In the West, the pharmaceutical industry has provided the answer. We call them anxiolytics, drugs that quiet or soothe our anxieties. We pop pills to tranquilize our runaway thoughts, drink cocktails before dinner, and add a sleep aid before bedtime, all in an effort to stop worrying and relax. It's a multibillion-dollar industry fueled by schedules without margin, a culture where success is valued over relationships, and Christians who are driven to do more and more for God's kingdom.

Worry has become PC. It's the politically correct, socially acceptable sin. We give it a place at our daily table because it's honorable to have a lot on our shoulders. Christians aren't immune. In fact, we compound our worries with guilt over feeling anxious. We delight in moaning about our heavy loads as if it's spiritual to be overworked for God.

We worry about our jobs. Our children. Our finances. Our future. Illness. The unknown. The unexpected. The expectations of others.

Need a recipe for a miserable day? Worry about what others think of you. *Do I fit in? Am I wearing the right clothes? Why can't I seem to know what to say? What will they think of my performance?*

What if I fail?

What if my children fail?

What if I can't pay the bills?

What if others don't like me?

What if, what if, what if?

Whatif?

Let's break it down. If a volcano has erupted, it's because something beneath the surface has been smoldering.

What is beneath the volcano of our anxieties?

And how does the gospel have anything to do with this? Is worry a symptom of gospel debt?

Absolutely. We've allowed our problems to look big in the presence of a little Jesus.

At a basic level, we worry when we're not in control. If outcomes were totally under our control, and we could influence the future to turn out exactly like we wanted, worry would cease to be a problem, wouldn't it?

When we are functioning in grace saturation, we understand that we stand perfect before our Father on the basis of the cross of Christ *alone*. Our relationship with God is an act of grace from beginning to end. We did nothing to merit his love. We didn't earn it, didn't deserve it. The gospel makes it clear. Our salvation is, from start to finish, an act of God.

It's the same way with our day-to-day experiences. Outcomes are in God's control. As a result of my salvation, I've been exalted into a relationship with God, a position known as sonship. Because of this, the rights of an heir are mine.

When I am worried, I take something out of God's hands and assume control. However, it is only *if* I'm in control that I should be worried.

I'll explain something in this chapter because we're just beginning this journey together. Later I'll refer to this over and over,

78

but for now let me explain what I mean by our reliance on false gospels. A false gospel is anything I rely upon to make myself more acceptable to God (other than the cross of Christ) or anything I use to excuse my bad behavior ("Understand, I'm a victim here," or "I'm not as bad as the next guy," or "Everybody else is doing it").

Many times the false gospel behind our anxieties can be defined by a single word: pride. It's the reliance on self, and we're going to see in future chapters that this one problem is behind so many of the symptoms of gospel debt.

Why is that?

Because when we walk in pride, we're blind to our own need. When we are feeling self-sufficient, we're not relying on God. When we're proud, we shut off the way to walk through a problem relying on God's grace. We don't ask for help because we don't see the need.

Many instances of anxiety have nothing to do with pride, and to accept a blanket explanation that pride is at the center of every worry is flippant and insensitive to many who have experienced deep hurts and suffer anxiety as a result. Sexual and physical abuse certainly fall into this category. The anxiety experienced in the wake of such horror should be worked out with a competent, Christian counselor.

But for those of us who fall into worry as a part of everyday life, we need to ask ourselves, as our guts churn and our minds spin on, "Who is on the throne in my life right now?" We need to shock ourselves with the realization that we've dethroned the Almighty.

For some, the deeper issue has more to do with unbelief. For those of us filled with self-doubt rather than self-sufficiency (pride), anxiety can be a real problem, and the end result is the same. We're worried because we're not relying on God, not believing what the Bible promises us concerning our situation. Fortunately, regardless of underlying cause (pride or unbelief), a solution can be found through insightful application of spiritual resuscitation. Just as surgeons turn to simple principles to assist patients out of oxygen debt (the ABCs of airway, breathing, and circulation), we can turn to the ABCs of *acknowledging* our need (laying aside our pride), *believing* the gospel promises, and *communion* (meditative time spent in God's presence, allowing time for the Word of God to impact and change our souls).

Ever heard of a café coronary? It's when someone (classically eating in a café) gets some food item lodged in the trachea or windpipe. With the airway closed, the patient remains in oxygen debt. Similarly, pride is the café coronary of faith. Without seeing our need, we remain in gospel debt, and our worry increases.

The second step after assuring an open airway is to make sure respiration takes place. That's why **B** is for *breathing*. Just because the airway is open doesn't mean oxygen will move into the lungs. And just because we've been challenged to lay aside our pride and acknowledge our need doesn't mean that we're going to exercise the faith needed to create a positive change in our life. That's why **B** is for *believe*. Believing the promises inherent in the gospel leads soul-sustaining grace into our lives.

After **B** comes **C**. Respiration might occur, and oxygen might get into the bloodstream, but oxygen won't get distributed to the body without *circulation*. That's the **C**.

In soul resuscitation, **C** stands for *communion*, the time spent in quiet meditation on the promises of God, giving a chance for every area of our lives to be exposed to the truth of the gospel promises.

It's often only when the symptoms of our anxiety become so acute that they interfere with our happiness that we begin to cry out for help, but in opening ourselves to a solution beyond our control, we've taken the first step toward a solution.

What would I suggest for Bob and Sally at a time of crisis? I'd suggest some passages for meditation. Fix your heart on Psalm 91. The whole chapter is wonderful. Consider verses 11 and 14.

> For he will command his angels concerning you
>   to guard you in all your ways.
> . . . .
> Because he holds fast to me in love, I will deliver him;
>   I will protect him, because he knows my name.

Here's another:

> The fear of man lays a snare,
>   but whoever trusts in the Lord is safe. (Proverbs 29:25)

I love this one from the book of Isaiah. Notice that he makes a peaceful soul-state contingent on laying aside our pride and trusting God.

> You keep him in perfect peace
>   whose mind is stayed on you,
>   because he trusts in you. (26:3)

May I make another suggestion? It isn't enough to read these words. Pray to the Father for the gift of faith, to make the verses alive to your soul. Then spend time in communion and meditation, allowing adequate time for your soul to soak in the presence of God and his Word. This is the essence of **C**, *communion*.

During a physical crisis, especially where there are airway concerns, the importance of a correct application of the ABCs cannot be overstated. Literally, a life hangs in the balance.

Do you understand the stakes when a Christian continuously dwells in a state of grace debt or gospel debt? Our effectiveness as a channel of God's love is hampered. This is no less critical than any life-or-death scenario that is played out in emergency rooms across America every day.

Here are additional verses that you should keep as a part of your armamentarium. Of course, with every assault of anxiety on our souls, there are specific issues. Safety. The future. Our children. Finances. A thoughtful hour with the Bible and a reliable concordance should assist you in finding specific answers to your individual concern. Here are key verses that deal with worry in general. Use these liberally to accomplish steps **B** and **C**.

A Scriptural Prescription

Do not be anxious about anything, but in everything by prayer and supplication with thanksgiving let your requests be made known to God. And the peace of God, which surpasses all understanding, will guard your hearts and your minds in Christ Jesus. (Philippians 4:6–7)

Therefore I tell you, do not be anxious about your life, what you will eat or what you will drink, nor about your body, what you will put on. Is not life more than food, and the body more than clothing? Look at the birds of the air: they neither sow nor reap nor gather into barns, and yet your heavenly Father feeds them. Are you not of more value than they? And which of you by being anxious can add a single hour to his span of life? And why are you anxious about clothing? Consider the lilies of the field, how they grow: they neither toil nor spin, yet I tell you, even Solomon in all his glory was not arrayed like one of these. But if God so clothes the grass of the field, which

82

today is alive and tomorrow is thrown into the oven, will he not much more clothe you, O you of little faith? Therefore do not be anxious, saying, "What shall we eat?" or "What shall we drink?" or "What shall we wear?" For the Gentiles seek after all these things, and your heavenly Father knows that you need them all. But seek first the kingdom of God and his righteousness, and all these things will be added to you.

Therefore do not be anxious about tomorrow, for tomorrow will be anxious for itself. Sufficient for the day is its own trouble. (Matthew 6:25–34)

Fear not, little flock, for it is your Father's good pleasure to give you the kingdom. (Luke 12:32)

Casting all your anxieties on him, because he cares for you. (1 Peter 5:7)

Fret not yourself because of evildoers,
    be not envious of wrongdoers!
For they will soon fade like the grass
    and wither like the green herb.

Trust in the Lord, and do good;
    dwell in the land and befriend faithfulness.
Delight yourself in the Lord,
    and he will give you the desires of your heart.
Commit your way to the Lord;
    trust in him, and he will act.
He will bring forth your righteousness as the light,
    And your justice as the noonday.

Be still before the Lord and wait patiently for him;
    fret not yourself over the one who prospers in his way,
    over the man who carries out evil devices! (Psalm 37:1–7)

8

LOSING CONTROL

Domesticating Jesus in Our Anger

THE NEXT DAY, behind the closed doors of his office, Bob Christian had a meltdown. Unlike Sally, Bob wasn't one to brood and internalize his stress in guilt or anxiety. Bob was more of a tornado-kind-of-guy. Emotions ran fast. Furious. And often his impulsive words or actions resulted in hurt that took years to heal.

He lost the contract he'd gone to St. Louis to rescue. Hurt, rejected, and misled, Bob's response was a red-faced expletive. He slammed the phone down on his desk and swatted a stack of papers into the air. He stood, pacing his office and kicking the trash can to send it clanging into the bookshelf.

With the stress of Sally's condition smoldering beneath the surface, it had taken a business failure to take the roof off of his anger.

His secretary's timid voice squeaked from behind his closed door. "Mr. Christian, is everything OK?"

Everything is not OK! My wife probably has cancer, I've just lost the biggest account of the year, and my wife is acting like missing her surgery is tantamount to missing our wedding. She told me to go! "Everything's fine," he replied, trying to control his voice. Through clenched teeth he continued, "Just fine." He opened the top drawer of his desk and lifted a small flask. After unscrewing the top, he let the golden liquid burn his throat.

Then he choked back emotions threatening to erupt again and dropped his head against his desk.

A Somali child soldier shoves his AK-47 into the face of a white photojournalist, who raises his hands in quick surrender.

Why?

Because there is nothing more dangerous than a child with a gun. Without a mature conscience, normal restraints are absent, and disastrous outcomes are the norm.

When I lived in Virginia, I treated a teenager who had been shot by his younger brother. The teen had retrieved his father's pistol from a locked cabinet and left the gun on the top of his dresser.

Tragic mistake.

His brother, a preschooler of about four, found the gun and when confronted by his older brother, held the gun out in front of him and said, "Bang, bang" as he squeezed the trigger.

From a distance of less than two feet, the bullet found its mark, passing into the upper abdomen of the teen.

The younger brother hadn't known the gun was loaded. Even if he had, I don't imagine that he had a proper idea of the destructive power of the weapon.

Forty-five minutes later, with the teen on the operating table and his abdomen open in front of me, I assessed the injuries, tracing the path of the bullet. In and out of the liver, in and out of the stomach, and into the tissue overlying the aorta, the largest artery in the body.

My own pulse quickened. A gunshot injury to the aorta is almost always fatal.

What is the most dangerous human emotion?

Anger.

Because with anger our control begins to lessen. The cap holding back negative responses is loosened. That's why I began this chapter with a story about a child with a gun. Not because the child exemplifies anger, but because anger uncapped can have the same explosive results. What happens when we loosen the cap holding anger in check?

Counterclockwise half a turn and we speak too freely.

Counterclockwise a full turn and we raise our voices.

Blow the cap off completely and we slam our fists against the wall.

Anger is not sin. What we do in response to anger often is. The Bible makes it clear that it is possible to be angry without sinning.

> Be angry, and do not sin;
> ponder in your own hearts on your beds, and be silent.
> (Psalm 4:4)

> Be angry and do not sin; do not let the sun go down on your anger, and give no opportunity to the devil. (Ephesians 4:26–27)

I love the overt way that James, the brother of Jesus, puts it in his epistle.

> Know this my beloved brothers: let every person be quick to hear, slow to speak, slow to anger; for the anger of man does not produce the righteousness of God. (James 1:19)

Over and over we see the exhortation to be slow to anger, and over and over God is revealed as one who is the model of restraint.

Whoever is slow to anger is better than the mighty,
  and he who rules his spirit than he who takes a city.
    (Proverbs 16:32)

Whoever is slow to anger has great understanding,
  but he who has a hasty temper exalts folly.
    (Proverbs 14:29)

Be not quick in your spirit to become angry, for anger lodges in the bosom of fools. (Ecclesiastes 7:9)

Good sense makes one slow to anger,
  and it is his glory to overlook an offense. (Proverbs 19:11)

Clearly, it's possible to get angry and not sin. As I thought back over my life to times when I experienced anger, I couldn't think of one positive example to write about. Too often, anger results in my speaking words that I later regret. Anger is a basic emotion, a consequence of physical pain or something just not going our way. Once I heard author and speaker Neil Anderson explain that anger often results from a blocked goal.

What does he mean? Simply that when our plans or expectations are thwarted, it is natural to experience anger. Perhaps you plan a nice, quiet dinner with your spouse, and your son or daughter invites the soccer team. You have a goal of catching a plane, and a police officer stops you for speeding. You're driving along following the truck in front of you at a reasonable distance when another driver cuts in.

How am I functioning out of gospel debt when I'm angry? What false gospels have I substituted for the real thing? Have I again made Jesus and his gospel small in the face of some inconvenience?

We become angry when something or someone interferes with something we assume is ours by right. If it's my right to read the paper quietly after work, I'll be tempted to be angry if the children play noisily in the same room. If it is my right to drive on smooth roads, I'll be upset if the way is potholed and bumpy.

The Bible teaches us that in and of ourselves we find nothing redeemable. In Romans 3, cited from Psalm 14, we read,

> None is righteous, no, not one;
>   no one understands;
>   no one seeks for God.
> All have turned aside; together they have become worthless;
>   no one does good,
>   not even one. (Romans 3:10–12)

In fact, I deserve far less than the perfect job, a convenient life, a quiet moment with the paper, and smooth roads. My sin (and the longer I've been a Christian, the more my understanding of my own depravity deepens) separated me from God and made me perfectly deserving of eternal hell. If I live my life according to the gospel, I won't hold any rights as absolute. Anything good that comes my way is a consequence of grace. Anything bad, well, I should be getting hell, so nothing quite compares with that.

If I find myself angry and tempted to lash out, in essence I'm saying that I'm not as bad as I really am. I deserve the thing that's being denied to me. I'm downplaying my need for the cross and shaking a fist in the face of the One who died to save me.

One very natural time to become angry is when evil touches our lives. From the dawn of civilization, man's tendency has been to respond to pain with an even bigger, more painful gift for the one who has wronged him. The law as set forth in Leviticus was actually a restraint from retaliating in an unequal manner. The response was only to be "an eye for an eye" or "a tooth for a tooth."

Jesus turns it all upside down when he asks us to love our enemies and to return good for evil. Loving the unlovely, the undeserved, is the essence of grace, favor granted regardless of merit. Jesus urges us to love, using the strongest language. Not a suggestion, a perhaps-you-should, but a command. "This is my commandment, that you love one another as I have loved you" (John 15:12). As members of his body, this love is to define us. "By this all people will know that you are my disciples, if you have love for one another" (John 13:35).

We are not asked to love independent of his input. We are only asked to be channels of the impulses that originate in his heart. Returning good in the face of evil is possible only if we are willing to be channels of God's love toward the world. We need to see our enemies through the eyes of the One who sent his Son to die for their sin.

It helps if we remember that we too are in need of grace. It has been well said that the ground is level at the foot of the cross. I am a sinner for whom Christ died. The brother I am tempted to hate, the brother who does evil against me, is one who is loved by God, one for whom Christ gave his life.

Choosing to let go of anger and to forgive instead isn't easy, but it is a path of certain reward. Letting go of anger is easier if we have learned that we also have angered others by our actions.

Anger management has become big business. Company leaders have realized that anger, improperly challenged, can lead to inefficient workers and an unhappy workplace.

Soul First Aid

So we're to be slow to anger and overlook offenses. How can the ABCs of soul first aid assist?

A. We won't find ourselves out of gospel debt until we've seen the mess we're in. So we *acknowledge* our need. "Help me, Father. It's not in me to not be angry toward. . . ." We need to see our Savior in his bigness. Savoring Christ in his reality quickly brings my problem into focus as the miniscule irritant that it likely is.

B. We need to lay down our reliance on false gospels. "It's my right to be angry. He should have known I wanted to ask her to the prom." Choose to *believe* the gospel. We don't really deserve any good thing.

I need to lay down my right to be angry about my circumstances or toward another. In doing so, I am laying down my pride—my desire to be in control—and am relying on God.

Does he not love you? Can you not see your circumstances, even those that result in your anger, as divinely orchestrated to mold you into the image of Christ? Every circumstance, every inconvenience has been filtered by his love. Nothing touches you that he has not allowed. Can you trust his love? Can you see that when we only cry for deliverance from our situation we are treating the Almighty as one who exists only to serve our needs, one who is there to serve up the right feelings of contentment at a moment's notice? Can we not realize that in his bigness, he is in control of our present situation, allowing every circumstance, designing an outcome that he has promised would work out for good?

For I am sure that neither death nor life, nor angels nor rulers, nor things present nor things to come, nor powers, nor height nor depth,

91

nor anything else in all creation, will be able to separate us from the love of God in Christ Jesus our Lord. (Romans 8:38–39)

C. There are few quick steps in spiritual transformation. And it's step **C** that is most often overlooked in the instant-gratification-oriented West. We need to spend time in *communion*, allowing the gospel promises to circulate and touch every area of our souls. It is prolonged time spent in the presence of God that facilitates the soul transformation that we long for and need. Unfortunately, time spent alone without an agenda is frowned upon in a society where work equals validity.

When I am alone with God, none of my accomplishments look impressive. All of the things by which I define myself are exposed as insignificant in the presence of God. Am I tempted to rely on my works to bolster my ego? In the presence of the One who can speak a word and create the world, my greatest accomplishments are naught.

How do I find my value in his presence?

My worth soars as I bask in the presence of his love for me. When I learn to define myself by this fact alone, I find that I have obtained a new standard by which to judge myself.

The next natural step is that we begin first judging our brother or sister by this same criterion. They are the beloved of God.

Sometimes in a physical emergency, there are things that precede the ABCs. Consider the special circumstances surrounding a person burned in a fire. First and foremost, the patient must be moved to a safe place to prevent further injury. Quickly the patient must be extracted from the scene of the fire so that the rescuer and the victim can assess the ABCs in a safe environment.

Anger is a fire. The potential for explosive consequences and injury loom as a real threat. Sometimes it is a top priority to remove ourselves from a stimulus of anger *before we react.* Away from the person or circumstance (as much as is possible) so that the situation isn't worsened.

Walk away. Count to ten. Or one hundred. Use any technique you can to safely extract yourself from the circumstance that threatens to explode.

Then, safely away from the problem, we do the ABCs.

I need help. Believe the gospel promises. Communion.

These are the keys to helping Jesus back onto the throne of our lives and out of the servant's quarters.

A Scriptural Prescription

Meditate on God's sovereignty. Ultimately he is responsible for the circumstances in our lives that have resulted in our angry emotions. He is the one who has numbered the hairs on our heads. Can we remind our souls that God is in the business of working every circumstance out for our good and lay aside our angry feelings and trust that God knows what we need to work the image of Christ in our life?

> And we know that for those who love God all things work together for good, for those who are called according to his purpose. For those whom he foreknew he also predestined to be conformed to the image of his Son, in order that he might be the firstborn among many brothers. And those whom he predestined he also called, and those whom he called he also justified, and those whom he justified he also glorified. (Romans 8:28–30)

> And do not fear those who kill the body but cannot kill the soul. Rather fear him who can destroy both soul and body in hell.

Are not two sparrows sold for a penny? And not one of them will fall to the ground apart from your Father. But even the hairs of your head are all numbered. (Matthew 10:28–30)

Emotion without Restraint

Anger without restraint is very dangerous. Like a child with a gun, waving it in the face of another without judgment or conscience.

What happened to my gunshot patient? As I traced the path of the bullet with my finger, I could feel the pulse of the aorta. The bullet missed by millimeters, insuring that my patient would live. I repaired the liver and stomach and breathed a prayer of thanks.

9

THE SECURITY OF SAMENESS

*Domesticating Jesus by Not Trusting
the One Who Holds the Future*

THE NEWS OF Sally's biopsy report hit her with hurricane force. Yes, she'd expected a diagnosis of cancer, felt she *deserved* to have cancer, came from a family with breast cancer. But when the surgeon said, "I'm afraid I have some bad news," Sally hugged her arms around her chest and slowly rocked back and forth on the exam table without speaking.

The surgeon looked at Sally and Bob. "It's cancer," he said, "but it's treatable."

Slowly, he outlined a treatment plan that included more surgery, radiation, and chemotherapy.

Everything was going to change. Immediately. And the therapy was going to go on for months.

Sally would need to take some time away from work.

Bob would need to curtail some of his business travel.

A family beach vacation would be put on hold. Plans to continue with the children in private school was no longer a given.

Suddenly someone had burst the bubble of perfect plans Sally had made for her future.

Riding home in silence, Sally's hand went to her breast. I'm not even going to look the same. Will Bob still find me attractive?

Change assaults us from every aspect of our lives. Age. Illness. Friends move away. A job is lost. A loved one dies. Change happens. And for most of us, it doesn't feel particularly pleasant. And again, it challenges our view of God and reveals just how big (or little) Jesus has become in our lives.

I feel particularly qualified to write on this subject.

Since Kris and I married, we've moved our household ten times. Next year we are doing it again. Number eleven, back from Kenya to the USA. After a year at home on furlough, we may be facing move twelve. And not just moving to a nicer neighborhood, making an upward move to a big, new house. We're talking around the world. Each move brings new challenges, new uncertainties. The kids have to deal with new schools. Friendships are formed. Relationships begin and end. We face new jobs. New coworkers. New employees.

Ask my wife what she would like more than anything else in the world and I can predict her answer: "To stay in the same place for thirty years." Make a nest. Put down roots.

The physical laws of the universe teach us that inertia is part of life.

Inertia? Yes. Remember? A body at rest tends to stay at rest. A body in motion tends to remain in motion.

Stability feels right.

But modern society pushes against it.

Look around at the gray-haired members of your congregation. If they have a few children, I can almost guarantee that they have loved ones scattered around the U.S., if not the world. Modern business dictates flexibility, adaptability, and a willingness to move around.

Moving isn't the only change we face, just the one with which I'm most familiar. There's also new relationship status. Dating. Engagement. Marriage. Too often, divorce.

A new pastor.

A new job.

A new school. New teachers. New classes.

Seasons. Spring becomes summer followed by fall and winter.

We are wired to like routines, some more than others. While some of us thrive on variety, we still have the consistencies in our lives that keep us sane and on track. We use the same brand of antiperspirant, fold our socks the same way, and keep the same underwear drawer year after year. We fall into routines without trying. We like sameness. It's comfortable.

Think back to your childhood. Perhaps your mother fixed the same pot roast dinner every Sunday.

My wife's mother did, and it's a great memory for her. Sunday after church saw the Jantzi family gathered around a table of roast and potatoes. Sameness means security. The ability to predict an outcome with regular success is important.

Watch what happens to a newly married couple. Two worlds collide. His and hers become theirs. Hers and mine become ours.

Add a messy baby without a normal respect for scheduled meals and bedtime. It's a recipe for stress with a capital *S*.

One of the problems with life is that, *by definition*, it is characterized by change. Within our 100 trillion individual cells, chemical reactions, the exchange of water, waste, and nutrients, is a constant. To stop change is death.

In larger life, change is inevitable. We change our minds. We meet new people. And then they change. And then we have to cope with our personal change *and* their change.

So if change is so inevitable, so woven into the fabric of life, why do we bristle at the thought?

Because change threatens our grip on life. We don't like not being in control.

Change brings insecurity about the future. And that can be scary. Change rarely affects two individuals the same exact way. So, mix two individuals with the same change, and the result will be conflict!

A good novel will pass this test: open to any random page and begin to read. Is a conflict front and center? You see, what we abhor in our personal life, we love in our fiction. Threaten your protagonist with conflict. When it looks like the conflict might resolve, add another complication! And then another and another until all hope is banished. And then deepen it one more time before rescuing the main character from the misery.

As a result of the conflict, something will happen to the protagonist: change! We call the journey the protagonist takes a character arc. Without change, the protagonist will be flat and boring.

By divine plan, each of us is on a spiritual character arc. Aren't you glad God doesn't allow us to stagnate? It's a preordained plan for molding us into the image of Christ:

For those whom he foreknew he also predestined to be conformed to the image of his Son, in order that he might be the firstborn among many brothers. And those whom

98

he predestined he also called, and those whom he called he also justified, and those whom he justified he also glorified. (Romans 8:29–30)

Do not be conformed to this world, but be transformed by the renewal of your mind, that by testing you may discern what is the will of God, what is good and acceptable and perfect. (Romans 12:2)

And we all, with unveiled face, beholding the glory of the Lord, are being transformed into the same image from one degree of glory to another. For this comes from the Lord who is the Spirit. (2 Corinthians 3:18)

OK, so in addition to all of the other changes we face in our lives, we have to deal with the process of sanctification, which in and of itself can be a stress.

So what prescription can we offer as a balm to soothe the pain of change?

As always, we begin by opening ourselves to intervention. **A** is admitting we have a need. It helps to recognize the gospel debt in our unhealthy reactions to change. If we find ourselves anxious, I suspect we haven't fully surrendered to the fact that we aren't in control and were never meant to be.

Some reminders may help us to embrace rather than resist change:

Change Is Inevitable

Just knowing you're not alone in a particular struggle can be huge in helping us to adapt. When we realize that it's part of life, we can find strength to press on.

Change Is Part of God's Plan for You

When we come to realize that circumstances are not random, that God is in fact in control and is orchestrating life to mold us into the image of his Son, change isn't so threatening. Believing this is part of step **B** in our soul resuscitation.

> And I am sure of this, that he who began a good work in you will bring it to completion at the day of Jesus Christ. (Philippians 1:6)

God Is the Unchanging Anchor within a Sea of Change

> Only one thing doesn't change—God himself.

> For I the Lord do not change. (Malachi 3:6)

> . . . the Father of lights with whom there is no variation or shadow due to change. (James 1:17)

> God is not man, that he should lie, or a son of man, that he should change his mind. Has he said, and will he not do it? Or has he spoken, and will he not fulfill it? (Numbers 23:19)

The implications for this knowledge are tremendous. He never goes back on his word, and his love for us remains a constant. This is the anchor upon which we cling as the seas around us are in constant turmoil or change.

The truth of the gospel is this: I have full access into God's presence because of the work of the cross. As this truth becomes reality to me, it becomes the stabilizing, unchanging foundation that helps me cope with the anxiety surrounding any change. I can face any change in my life as long as the biggest, central issue of my soul's past, present, and future has been settled.

Only Passin' Through

Knowing that this earth is not my home gives me courage to face change. While my present is in a quandary of change, my future is secure. Look at the descriptions of believers in the New Testament. Words like *exiles*, *aliens*, and *sojourners* are given to us.

Let's face it. We weren't made for this fallen world. And as a result, we're never going to quite "fit." There will always be a longing for something more.

This is not our home. When I am facing yet another move as a missionary, from the U.S. to Africa and back, I remind myself that one day I will find my permanent sanctuary in Heaven. Short of that, I have to accept the inevitability of change.

God never intended us to set our hearts on this earth as our treasure. Frequently I remind myself, *I'm only passin' through*.

Conduct yourselves with fear throughout the time of your exile. (1 Peter 1:17)

I love the way the *God's Word* translation reads in the same verse: "Live your time as temporary residents on earth."

Beloved, I urge you as sojourners and exiles to abstain from the passions of the flesh, which wage war against your soul. (1 Peter 2:11)

> Do not lay up for yourselves treasures on earth, where moth and rust destroy and where thieves break in and steal, but lay up for yourselves treasures in heaven, where neither moth nor rust destroys and where thieves do not break in and steal. For where your treasure is, there your heart will be also. (Matthew 6:19–21)

So much of the treatment for this problem addresses the problem of anxiety that surrounds change. We worry because we do not know the outcome. God's grace toward us is unchanging. Knowing that, really *believing* that, will give us the flexibility to face change without breaking.

So much of the problem with change is how it affects our future. Our plans and dreams have to change too. And that can be a major problem.

The future. For most of us, it's spelled with a capital *F*, and we'd give anything to know what's around the bend.

Our society is fascinated with the future. We love futuristic movies and sci-fi; Hollywood tickles our minds with the idea. Wouldn't it be great to know what the future holds?

Remember a TV show that was popular a few years ago, *Early Edition*? It was all about a guy who got tomorrow's paper delivered mysteriously to his door every morning. And every day he'd go about trying to prevent some tragedy that he knew was going to happen in the future.

If you had an opportunity to glimpse the future, say, what your life would be like in ten or twenty years, would you take it?

Fortunately, my question is hypothetical. It's not going to happen. At least not the way we'd like.

Questions about our future are a major source of anxiety throughout life and are some of the anxieties that reveal just how domesticated Jesus has become to us. That's why I decided to devote a bit of space to it here.

Whom will I marry? Where will I attend school, college, or university? What job will I get? Will I still be in this same job? What will my children be like? What will they study? Will we ever move? Will we ever stop moving and settle down? Will my health hold up? Will my retirement investments be enough? Will the market go up or down? Will I make the grade? Win the race?

Missionaries aren't immune from this sort of worry. If anything, the temptation is more acute because the stakes are so high. *Am I called to serve in _____? Will my support be enough? Where will I live during furlough? How will I travel to give updates to supporting churches? Will the government continue to look favorably on my request for a longer visa? Will we ever see a convert from these stubborn people? How long should we stay on the field before returning to our home supporters? When should we return? Should we return? What does the future hold?*

I remember a few years ago climbing Mt. Kenya with my family. To make the summit by sunrise, you leave the protection of camp at 3 AM. There are two reasons for this. First, it's still so cold that most of the small pebbles are frozen to the slope, so it's easier to climb without constantly sliding back down. The second reason is that in the dark *you can't see how steep and how far the journey is.* Your flashlight provides a small circle of light to guide you a step at a time. You see only the ground and the back of the hiker in front of you. Seeing the summit could be inspiring . . . or discouraging. *I have to climb up there?*

A few years ago I researched a series of novels about a woman whose father has Huntington's disease. Huntington's disease is inherited from a parent and doesn't reveal itself in symptoms until midlife, usually around thirty-five. The illness is quite devastating, causing a loss of voluntary muscle control, a condition that is progressive and results in constant dance-like movements of the arms and legs. Eventually the victims can't control themselves at all and are confined to bed and wheelchair. In the end, swallowing control is interrupted, and often the patients will choke, often culminating in pneumonia and death.

What interested me about the disease was that it is a genetic illness, present in the DNA from the moment of conception but not expressed until later in life, often after life's plans have been set. Careers are begun. Marriage and children often precede the onset of the illness. By the time the patient starts to twitch, the gene may have already been passed to the next generation.

My protagonist felt a call to be in surgery but then discovered that she might be carrying the Huntington's disease gene. The crux of the issue rose to the surface: Could my protagonist trust the God who created her and formulated her DNA according to his plan, even if she carried the HD gene and it would ruin her career?

As I was researching the topic, I ran across a little book called *Deceived by God?* It told the heart-wrenching story about a man and woman who desired to serve as missionaries in a foreign country. As it turned out, unbeknownst to the husband, the woman he'd married had the HD gene. Neither he nor his wife knew that the HD gene was in the family. He hypothesized that God, in his sovereign wisdom, kept the information back from him, so that he would proceed forward with marriage.

One Step at a Time: The Essence of Faith

I've often been intrigued by the promise in the Psalms that the Word of God will be our guide: "Your word is a lamp to my feet and a light to my path" (119:105).

"A lamp to my feet" implies guidance for only a few steps ahead. Could this mean that God will commonly only provide information enough for the next step?

Isn't this the whole crux of the Christian life? We are to walk by faith, not by far-viewing sight. *There are few signs declaring the distance to our destination beside the narrow road.*

So why does my soul bristle at not knowing?

Is it not because I have not learned to trust his love?

Am I so addicted to control (or the illusion that I'm in control) that my heart quickens with anxiety when I am faced with unknown door number two?

Just what does walking in faith mean in regard to the future? Do we throw away our plans?

Of course not. James says we make plans understanding that everything is subject to his sovereign will.

> Come now, you who say, "Today or tomorrow we will go into such and such a town and spend a year there and trade and make a profit"—yet you do not know what tomorrow will bring. What is your life? For you are a mist that appears for a little time and then vanishes. Instead you ought to say, "If the Lord wills, we will live and do this or that." (James 4:13–15)

It's not wrong to ask for God to reveal his way. But it is wrong to be anxious about tomorrow.

> Therefore I tell you, do not be anxious about your life, what you will eat or what you will drink, nor about your body, what you will put on. . . . Therefore do not be anxious about tomorrow, for tomorrow will be anxious for itself. Sufficient for the day is its own trouble. (Matthew 6:25, 34)

Prescription for Freedom from Gospel Debt

Let's face it. The gospel debt in our anxiety about the future isn't hard to see. The cure is to go back to the basics of the gospel and review God's promises again. Here's what's in the first aid kit to treat future uncertainty. *Acknowledge* your need. *Believe. Commune* with the Scriptures to give them a chance to penetrate your weary (and sometimes hardened) soul. This is only a starting point. Be sure to take the whole dose to lessen your chances of a relapse!

For I know the plans I have for you, declares the Lord, plans for welfare and not for evil, to give you a future and a hope. (Jeremiah 29:11)

"For the mountains may depart
  and the hills be removed,
but my steadfast love shall not depart from you,
  and my covenant of peace shall not be removed,"
  says the Lord, who has compassion on you.
    (Isaiah 54:10)

And I am sure of this, that he who began a good work in you will bring it to completion at the day of Jesus Christ. (Philippians 1:6)

Mark the blameless and behold the upright,
  for there is a future for the man of peace. (Psalm 37:37)

Let not your heart envy sinners,
  but continue in the fear of the Lord all the day.
Surely there is a future,
  and your hope will not be cut off. (Proverbs 23:17–18)

O afflicted one, storm-tossed and not comforted,
  behold, I will set your stones in antimony,
  and lay your foundations with sapphires.
I will make your pinnacles of agate,
  your gates of carbuncles,
  and all your wall of precious stones.
All your children shall be taught by the Lord,
  and great shall be the peace of your children.
In righteousness you shall be established;
  you shall be far from oppression, for you shall not fear;
  and from terror, for it shall not come near you.
. . . .
no weapon that is fashioned against you shall succeed,
  and you shall confute every tongue that rises against you
      in judgment.
This is the heritage of the servants of the Lord
  and their vindication from me, declares the Lord.
      (Isaiah 54:11–14, 17)

Psalm 91 (The whole thing!)

They are to do good, to be rich in good works, to be generous
and ready to share, thus storing up treasure for themselves as
a good foundation for the future, so that they may take hold
of that which is truly life. (1 Timothy 6:18–19)

For I am sure that neither death nor life, nor angels nor rulers, nor things present nor things to come, nor powers, nor
height nor depth, nor anything else in all creation, will be able
to separate us from the love of God in Christ Jesus our Lord.
(Romans 8:38–39)

Let not your hearts be troubled. Believe in God; believe also
in me. In my Father's house are many rooms. If it were not

so, would I have told you that I go to prepare a place for you? And if I go and prepare a place for you, I will come again and will take you to myself, that where I am you may be also. (John 14:1–3)

And your ears shall hear a word behind you, saying, "This is the way, walk in it," when you turn to the right or when you turn to the left. (Isaiah 30:21)

And the Lord will guide you continually
    and satisfy your desire in scorched places
    and make your bones strong;
and you shall be like a watered garden,
    like a spring of water,
      whose waters do not fail. (Isaiah 58:11)

10

YAWNING IN THE PRESENCE OF A MIGHTY GOD

The Reason We Are Complacent in Sunday Worship

ON SUNDAY, Bob and Sally sat in their normal spot, two-thirds of the way back, left side. It was a comfortable routine.

Sally listened with one ear to the sermon and one ear to her own distracted thoughts. Reverend Smith spoke on living a positive life, a feel-good-about-yourself message that had become his weekly mantra. He told a nice story about a man surviving at sea alone. Powerful stuff about man's will to live in the face of trouble.

But he didn't open the source of life, the Word of God.

Sally shifted in her seat and studied the other members of the congregation. Mr. Roberts was asleep. Mrs. Simone was reading the bulletin. Others nodded their approval of the message.

But Sally knew too much. Victor Jones sat smugly on his wallet. He'd given enough money to the church to build a new fellowship hall and insure himself that the Reverend would never question his affair with his secretary. In front of Mr. Jones, Randy Bransfield was planning his business week. His wife was planning the menu for the garden club.

Most of the flock seemed content to give God this hour. It fit neatly into their upper-middle-class life, as long as Reverend Smith made them feel OK about the country-club Christianity they'd perfected.

Meanwhile, Sally felt guilty. Because of her current illness, she felt a real need to get serious with God. She wanted healing. But she didn't dare ask. Besides the fact that she was convinced that she was being punished, she just couldn't bring herself to the humble position of baring her soul to the socialites who gathered week by week.

Instead, Sally sat in silence and put forward a strong front.

For a moment imagine with me a starving man. He's gone weeks without food, and his skin is stretched tight over bony prominences that used to be padded with healthy flesh. In addition, he's gone hours without water. His mouth is desert-sand dry. Then he is rescued and placed at a banquet table.

What would we think if he turned away, uninterested in the nourishment that could save him? What if he sat at the table and contented himself with another activity, say, reading a book, rather than quenching his thirst?

It is unthinkable that his hunger and thirst would not drive him to put all other pursuits on hold until he satisfied the demands for food and drink.

How is it that so often I can't see my own wretched need, the desperate state of my soul, and end up coming into the presence of God not even hungry for change?

The wretchedness of my fallen state and the provision of Christ and his gospel are so abundant that it doesn't even compare

110

to a starving man at a banquet. My need and his provision make my example a mere shadow of the reality of me approaching the throne of grace.

So why can't I see my need? How is it that I can be complacent when I come together with other Christians in Sunday morning worship?

Jesus made it clear. There is a manifestation of his presence in a gathering of believers that is different than what we can experience on our own. Of course, his presence is always with us. We believe that the Holy Spirit is indwelling our lives, and we should regularly spend time just with God alone. But together there is something special. "For where two or three are gathered in my name, there am I among them" (Matthew 18:20).

Mature Christians aren't immune. It seems that when I'm doing well in my Christian life, being used in ministry to others, the first temptation is for me to see less of my need and to rest on my own righteousness. That's pitiful. But that's human nature. We mentally pat ourselves on the back for something the Bible calls "filthy rags" (Isaiah 64:6, NIV). That's what our best is in comparison to Christ's righteousness.

So what's the problem with us? How is it that we fail to come into a gathering of the body of Christ with awe, expectation, excitement, and maybe a healthy dose of fear?

In my surgical way of looking at things (surgeons tend to enjoy simple explanations rather than long convoluted solutions), I'd like to suggest that two basic problems keep us from a proper mental posture on Sunday mornings. Number one: I've allowed myself to become too big. Number two: I've allowed Jesus to become too small.

Sound familiar? It should. It's the essence of domesticating Jesus.

111

Let me explain. The first problem in my mental dullness when approaching the throne of grace stems from my own blindness to my need. This is defined by one ugly word: pride. When pride is in operation, I don't see my own wretchedness, my own hunger, and so I walk by the banquet table without appreciating it.

1. Pride

Kadijah Abul Osman was too young for cancer. But when the doctor looked at the X-ray of her arm and frowned, she felt a knot forming in her stomach. He called over a second physician and pointed to a dark spot on the film. "Here," he said, as if she couldn't hear. "It looks like a tumor."

A tumor? She shook her head. *Cancer?* The pain in her right arm had been constant for the last month. Not horrible, but too much to excuse away as a strain from carrying firewood.

The doctor walked back from the X-ray view box. "We need to do a biopsy of the bone in your arm."

"A biopsy?"

"Take a little bit of the bone to analyze."

"Do I have cancer?"

The doctor looked away. She didn't like that.

Why won't he look at me?

"We just need to do a test so we can know." He shrugged. "It's probably nothing."

But *nothing* didn't require her to come back for an operation. A real operation where she'd be put to sleep and everything.

She nodded resolutely. "You're the doctor."

The biopsy was performed by an orthopedic surgeon two weeks later. And a week after that, she was back in the clinic at Kijabe Hospital to find out the biopsy results.

She sat in the crowded waiting room trying not to dwell on the negative possibilities. *If it's cancer, they will have to amputate my arm.*

A few minutes later, she studied the face of the physician in front of her, trying to discern the news.

He looked at the pathologist's report of her biopsy and smiled. "Fascinating," he said. He nodded. "Good news."

She swallowed, unable to speak.

"I think you have a tumor."

"I have cancer?"

"No, the biopsy of your bone is negative for cancer. It's called a brown tumor."

"What do you need to do?"

"I need to send you to a general surgeon. I want him to operate on your neck."

"What?" *The problem is in my arm!* "But my arm—"

"Let me draw a picture so you can understand," he said. He drew the outline of a person and put four small dots in the neck. "Here," he said, pointing to the spots, "you have four parathyroid glands. These glands regulate your calcium levels in the blood. When your calcium level is low, the glands secrete a hormone that tells your bones to give up calcium into the blood, by activating special cells called osteoclasts."

She stared at the picture. She didn't get it.

"In your case, I believe there must be a tumor on one of the little glands, causing an overproduction of the hormone responsible for the bones giving up the calcium. The excess hormone caused the osteoclasts in your arm to be overactive. They formed a cyst in your bone in order to raise the blood calcium level."

"That's what was in my arm?"

"Exactly. I need to do a lab test to see how high the parathyroid hormone level is."

Two weeks later, Kadijah was in my clinic holding a lab slip revealing one of the highest parathyroid levels I'd seen in years.

"We'll have to operate," I said, "and search the neck to find the tumor responsible for the high hormone level."

"And what if you don't operate?"

"Your bones will continue to weaken. Your calcium levels will continue to rise. Eventually it could cause heart problems." I paused before adding, "Even death."

Primary hyperparathyroidism is the fancy name given to describe Kadijah's condition. And yes, a tumor of a tiny gland in the neck is the culprit. A little gland in the neck called the parathyroid gland stops obeying the rules and begins to grow, and one by one the weird symptoms begin to appear.

In medical school we used a little rhyme to help us remember the complaints associated with high calcium levels that go with this fancy diagnosis: stones (in the kidney), bones (osteoporosis and tumors like Kadijah's), abdominal groans (gastritis and ulcers), and psychiatric moans (psychosis can occur as the calcium levels get extremely high).

The disease is a fascinating one. Why? Because although the presenting problem is in the arm, it takes a knowledge of physiology to pinpoint the source of the malfunction. The parathyroid tumor is causing no local neck symptoms, but is happily wreaking havoc with multiple other systems.

Pride is like that. It will rarely come right out and proclaim, "Here I am. Deal with me." Instead it raises its ugly head in a myriad of other symptoms. Look back through the chapters in this book. So many can be manifestations of pride. And so, even though we've touched on it in other chapters, I want to concentrate on this specific diagnosis now because it's one that affects us all. And the symptoms pop up in so many unexpected ways.

I get anxious when I've slipped into the driver's seat of my life, urged into this position by the prideful assumption that I'm capable of taking the wheel.

I get angry or bitter if, in my pride, I take on God's role as judge.

Guilt reveals my subtle pride because I am astonished that I am capable of falling yet again.

I get critical when others can't see things my way. Ugly pride.

I get impatient when someone delays *my* agenda. Oops, pride again.

I sit in the presence of God and remain unmoved by his grace . . . because I don't see my own wretchedness.

So, just like focusing on the arm of a patient with a brown tumor isn't going to solve the problem, sometimes attacking the peripheral symptom associated with pride isn't going to get rid of the bothersome symptom.

Remember what we said about a café coronary? It's when a victim dies of choking on a bite of food. It's due to airway obstruction and isn't really a coronary, but the person dies suddenly because of a lack of oxygen.

In our metaphor using the ABCs of resuscitation, **A** is for airway, and establishing a clear airway is always priority one. Without it (that is, with a closed or obstructed airway), oxygen can't get in, and death will occur within minutes.

Pride has been called the café coronary of our faith. Why? Because with pride we never see our need, and so we never acknowledge our need of grace. With pride we rarely get beyond step one, because we remain blind to our need of grace.

So if we're proud and we're blind to it, how will we ever be healed?

By recognizing the subtle clues.

Anxiety, criticism, impatience, anger, and guilt to name a few.

115

One of the indications that we've slipped into pride is a lack of gratitude. A characteristic of the humble heart is the profound thankfulness that flows from a heart that knows it doesn't deserve blessing. On the contrary, when we begin to think, *Hey, I've earned this*, we don't tend to be thankful.

Some symptoms of pride are less than subtle. I used to get the news magazine of a popular ministry in the United States. But with each edition I noticed the prominence of the leader's pictures . . . almost on every page. I'll admit, I developed a bit of a bad attitude toward this particular man, and every time I got the newsletter, I counted his picture, and every time I came away with the question, who is being praised . . . the cross, or the ministry's leader?

To gain a little insight into the prescription for the treatment of pride, let's look at the Bible.

Humble yourselves before the Lord, and he will exalt you. (James 4:10)

Likewise, you who are younger, be subject to the elders. Clothe yourselves, all of you, with humility toward one another, for "God opposes the proud but gives grace to the humble." Humble yourselves, therefore, under the mighty hand of God so that at the proper time he may exalt you. (1 Peter 5:5–6)

The Bible's answer to pride? "Humble yourselves."

Like that's easy when you're struggling with pride!

I didn't say it would be easy. But it's so worth it. So just how do you humble yourself?

Look back at the verses we read in 1 Peter. In *Today's English Version* verse 5 reads, "Put on the apron of humility, to serve one another." I love that picture. Humility has something to do with serving others. Pride has something to do with wanting others to serve us.

Christ is our example here.

> Do nothing from rivalry or conceit, but in humility count others more significant than yourselves. Let each of you look not only to his own interests, but also to the interests of others. Have this mind among yourselves, which is yours in Christ Jesus, who, though he was in the form of God, did not count equality with God a thing to be grasped, but made himself nothing, taking the form of a servant, being born in the likeness of men. And being found in human form, he humbled himself by becoming obedient to the point of death, even death on a cross. (Philippians 2:3–8)

> It shall not be so among you. But whoever would be great among you must be your servant, and whoever would be first among you must be your slave, even as the Son of Man came not to be served but to serve, and to give his life as a ransom for many. (Matthew 20:26–28)

We can begin to see practically what humbling means.

To Be Humble Means to Serve Others

I love the passage in John 13 where Jesus is with his disciples to celebrate the Feast of the Passover. Pay particular attention to how John sets it up. "Jesus, knowing that the Father had given all things into his hands, and that he had come from God and was going back to God, rose from supper" (vv. 3–4).

OK, John, I get it. Jesus knew who he was, where he'd come from, and where he was going. He knew he was God incarnate, the one worthy of the worship of the universe. So what does he do? "He laid aside his outer garments, and taking a towel, tied it around his waist. Then he poured water into a basin and began to wash the disciples' feet and to wipe them with the towel that was wrapped around him" (vv. 4–5)

The essence of a life lived in the fullness of our great salvation is a life lived in freedom from the service of self. Paul says it this way: "For you were called to freedom, brothers. Only do not use your freedom as an opportunity for the flesh, but through love serve one another" (Galatians 5:13).

To Be Humble Means to Obey . . . Someone Else

In Philippians it says that Jesus humbled himself "by becoming obedient." Humility accepts someone else's will. Pride accepts its own agenda and follows it.

Humility Means Coming as a Child

Over and over Jesus spoke of the necessity of coming like a child.

> And calling to him a child, he put him in the midst of them and said, "Truly, I say to you, unless you turn and become like children, you will never enter the kingdom of heaven. Whoever humbles himself like this child is the greatest in the kingdom of heaven." (Matthew 18:2–4)

So what are children like? They certainly haven't accomplished much. They're too young for that, and so they aren't tempted to rest on their accomplishments. A key characteristic is that children are naturally *trusting*.

So, if you're suspicious that pride is hiding beneath any of a myriad of symptoms in your life, the cure is to humble yourself. That is, we're to trust, obey, and serve.

It seems ironic to proclaim that the cure for pride is as simple as humbling yourself. After all, pride is an attitude, right? Can a cure be found in following simple actions?

I think so. As we take on the posture of service and participate in acts of humble service, God deals a heavy blow to our own pride.

When a symptom is always associated with a particular diagnosis, we call that symptom pathognomonic for the disease. For pride, the pathognomonic symptom would be boasting, something for which a reliance on the true gospel has no room.

> For by grace you have been saved through faith. And this is not your own doing; it is the gift of God, not a result of works, so that no one may boast. (Ephesians 2:8–9)

> For if I preach the gospel, that gives me no ground for boasting. (1 Corinthians 9:16)

There is one exception for boasting.

> But far be it from me to boast except in the cross of our Lord Jesus Christ, by which the world has been crucified to me, and I to the world. (Galatians 6:14)

Pride Boasts in Strength; Humility Boasts in Weakness

The essence of a life lived in the fullness of grace, the fullness of this great salvation, is a life of love, where we stand humbled by the acceptance of unmerited and unconditional love and where that love spills into the needy world around us. In the presence of such great love, our boasting is silenced. Paul teaches us about love in 1 Corinthians 13 where we read that

> Love is patient and kind; love does not envy or boast; is not arrogant or rude. It does not insist on its own way. (1 Corinthians 13:4–5)

A weakness in the apostle Paul is responsible for the precious words we find in 2 Corinthians:

> But he said to me, "My grace is sufficient for you, for my power is made perfect in weakness." Therefore I will boast all the more gladly of my weaknesses, so that the power of Christ may rest upon me. For the sake of Christ, then, I am content with weaknesses, insults, hardships, persecutions, and calamities. For when I am weak, then I am strong. (2 Corinthians 12:9–10)

Sadly, even when God clearly does something through us, we have to fight the tendency toward pride. Even if we acknowledge that God did the work, we fight the subtle tendency to be proud that he decided to use us. When our eyes are open to this, we see it as ridiculous as a glass being proud that it can quench thirst just because it held the water!

> But we have this treasure in jars of clay, to show that the surpassing power belongs to God and not to us. (2 Corinthians 4:7)

By now, I'm sure you've seen the trend. Victory over gospel debt is found in a celebration of our inability!

Fight it on your own, in your own strength, and you'll be fighting pride with . . . pride!

Embrace your weakness and rely on his power, and you'll find yourself in the right place: humbled at the foot of the cross.

The ABCs

We've seen the problem with pride in its manifold symptoms that surface in so many ways. We've also noted the difficulty in making a diagnosis because the problem of pride itself prevents us from seeking help.

For this reason I'd suggest keeping an open mind about pride. Realize that even mature Christians flip in and out of self-reliance just about as easy as they breathe. Knowing this, we should *stay alert* and be suspicious of the pride that is lurking just under the surface.

When a patient comes to me with an area of skin that is swollen, painful, and red, I'm not content to apply an antibiotic salve or even just to prescribe an antimicrobial. I am immediately suspicious that a pocket of infection is lurking below the surface (an abscess) and will go untreated without surgical intervention.

So it is with pride. When we've hit a stall in our spiritual growth, when our joy has vanished, when we find ourselves dry, or angry or feeling guilty, or we've just plain lost a sense of awe in the presence of God . . . we should suspect that an abscess of pride is hiding beneath the surface. Take the scalpel of humility, and drain the problem straightaway because treating the surface symptom won't result in a cure.

So the first problem is in making a firm diagnosis. **A**. Once it is suspected, quickly acknowledge your need of grace and your tendency to want to fight this in your own strength. **B**. Then go back over the truth of the gospel, that wonderful story of our redemption in spite of our wretchedness. Ask God to help you believe the truth and to realize the incredible fallout that results from being his child. **C.** Spend time in communion in God's presence. There, in the presence and realization of his glory, our accomplishments are seen as miniscule and our temptation to pride is reduced.

I operated on Kadijah, exploring her neck and removing a huge parathyroid tumor. Perhaps I shouldn't use the word "huge" lest you think I removed a cantaloupe-sized mass. *Huge* is a relative term here. What I removed was about the size of three large grapes. Normally a parathyroid gland is much smaller than an eraser on the end of a pencil.

Once the offending gland was out of the way, the hormone level returned to normal, and her bones began to strengthen again.

It's amazing how effective it is to eliminate the problem when you attack the source!

2. Something Else Has Taken Over the Number One Treasure Spot

Number two?

Yes, remember, we were talking about the two main problems in our dullness as we gather on Sunday mornings. The first problem was pride; that is, we've allowed ourselves to be too big. The second is that Jesus has gotten too small to enthrall our hearts.

In essence, that's what this whole book has been about, but let me offer some directed thoughts here.

When a surgeon searches for a diagnosis, he looks first at clues. A main source of clues is the patient's history. To what diagnosis are the symptoms pointing?

One of the first symptoms that something other than Jesus has taken over the number one treasure spot in our hearts is discontentment. In truth, nothing can satisfy like Jesus. But that doesn't seem to quell our tendency to seek satisfaction outside of Christ. The Old Testament prophet Jeremiah says we should be shocked at this:

> Be appalled, O heavens, at this;
>> be shocked, be utterly desolate,
>>> declares the Lord,
> for my people have committed two evils:
> they have forsaken me,
>> the fountain of living waters,
> and hewed out cisterns for themselves,
>> broken cisterns that can hold no water.
>> (Jeremiah 2:12–13)

That's pretty much the drum I've been beating throughout this whole book. I should be appalled that I'm not content with the Lord of the Universe. That's because I've domesticated him into something that can slip from the top spot.

I think I have an advantage over some of you. Right now I'm living in East Africa, working out of a mission hospital in Kenya. Although I am exposed to a certain amount of advertising, I'm sheltered from the avalanche of ads that threaten to bury most of you in the West.

The messages may be different, but the underlying communication carries a restrain of discontent. *Buy me. Drive me. Eat me. You're not good enough unless . . .*

New is better. Bigger. Faster. More powerful.

Is it really important to have two hundred horsepower to drive the kids to school?

Do we have to wear the latest style with a designer logo?

Is TV really so much more enjoyable if the screen is a few inches wider?

Or is it just the same old Hollywood drivel and we've swallowed the advertising lie?

A good friend, a career missionary in Africa, recently bemoaned a conversation she'd had with a woman back home.

The woman clasped her hand around a jeweled necklace. "I just couldn't participate in short-term foreign missions. It's not safe."

"We're careful," my friend said. "We don't go out at night, and we don't wear expensive jewelry that might make us a target."

"That's just it. I couldn't go three weeks without my jewelry."

Wow, I thought. *Did she realize how shallow she sounded?*

In some ways, living in a developing country has sharpened the focus in my mind. Just because I'm white, most Africans assume I have money. The next assumption is the most dangerous: because I have money, I must be content.

How do you fill in the sentence? I'd be content if only

_____.

We all have to fight this one. All of us, from the poorest-of-the-poor homeless child to the wealthiest tycoon. There's always the feeling that a little more will change everything. Satisfaction will come. We'll be able to relax. I just need a little more. Conversely, after I've visited the mud-walled home of a traditional Maasai tribesman, I've often thought that more stuff definitely doesn't mean more contentment.

It reminds me of the old joke (before there were government rules about such activity): How many Kenyans can fit in a *matatu* (the common public transportation vans)? One more.

I heard a wise man say that the secret of happiness is wanting what you have, not what you don't. Hmmm.

The truth of the matter is easy to say, and hard to digest and implement. God never promised us financial blessings in return for our love.

But he did promise us that his grace would be enough to sustain us regardless of circumstances.

Slow down long enough to get off the rat-race wheel and ask yourself if you are really happier because of the last item that you just had to have. Or once the excitement and newness wore off, were you just as restless as before?

The truth is this: God never intended for us to find satisfaction outside of himself. On this side of eternity, God has provided many things for our pleasure, but none are to provide the complete satisfaction available in God himself.

Is it wrong to desire purposeful work, clothing for protection from the environment, and food for supper?

Of course not. That's the way we've been created. But when it comes to wanting a faster car, a bigger house, or a computer with all the latest bells and whistles, the answer might be different.

It should prompt us to take a look at our soul life. Are we functioning in an appropriate amount of grace saturation, or have we slipped into gospel debt and our discontentment is only a symptom of our reliance on a false gospel?

Perhaps we need to spend a little time remembering who we are as a result of the gospel and remembering the priority of his calling in our lives to be channels of gospel-love to others.

I am a son of the most high God. An inheritance beyond earthly comprehension awaits me at my death. He has called me to a life of sacrifice and service, a life where I can gladly lay aside my desires for creature comforts for the sake of his fame, a life where true joy and contentment is found in seeing others come to the place where God is treasured as he should be.

When my neighbor looks at me, what does he or she see? A man so enamored by the love of God that I can't help talking about him and the wonder that he's forgiven me? Or a man in love with stuff?

Have we become men who wax our Harleys longer than we stand in worship? Do we spend more time purchasing designer-labeled clothing so that we will be treasured or on activities that reflect that God himself is our all in all?

Spiritual First Aid

The ABCs are the same regardless of the source of the oxygen debt. Likewise, our spiritual first aid begins with the same priorities. Are we in grace debt?

We begin with a quick assessment of our receptivity to help. Are we standing in our own strength, relying in our own abilities to handle our problems? *I'm not really that bad. Everyone struggles with this. I can handle it.* When we've come to the point of understanding that we are helpless to save ourselves, we find that we've taken the first step in acknowledging our need. We see we can't make it on our own. The pride blocking the graceway is extracted, and we're ready to breathe in the true gospel.

Next we take a look at the promises that come as part of the gospel explosion fallout. There is a difference between a mental nod at the truth of these promises and a heart-belief. Meditate on these promises that document our present standing as heirs of God, as his sons and daughters, and as his bride. Then ask God to give you the gift of faith to believe what he has promised.

C means spending time in communion with those promises. Ask God where you might need a little extra effort. What verses should I memorize that will help me with this problem in the future?

When I see a patient in the emergency room, the ABCs are assessed within the first moments. When it comes to making a definitive plan, often a prescription medication will be added to assist the patient forward in the coming weeks. Our prescription for contentment might look something like this. "Meditate on these passages daily until discontentment ceases."

Not that I am speaking of being in need, for I have learned in whatever situation I am to be content. I know how to be brought low, and I know how to abound. In any and every circumstance, I have learned the secret of facing plenty and hunger, abundance and need. I can do all things through him who strengthens me. (Philippians 4:11–13)

Now there is great gain in godliness with contentment, for we brought nothing into the world, and we cannot take anything out of the world. But if we have food and clothing, with these we will be content. But those who desire to be rich fall into temptation, into a snare, into many senseless and harmful desires that plunge people into ruin and destruction. For the love of money is a root of all kinds of evils. It is through this craving that some have wandered away from the faith and pierced themselves with many pangs. (1 Timothy 6:6–10)

Keep your life free from love of money, and be content with what you have, for he has said, "I will never leave you nor forsake you." (Hebrews 13:5)

I can't read that last verse without conviction. What right do I have to wallow in discontentment when I've been awarded with his abiding presence?

And because you are sons, God has sent the Spirit of his Son into our hearts, crying, "Abba! Father!" So you are no longer a slave, but a son, and if a son, then an heir through God. (Galatians 4:6–7)

Blessed be the God and Father of our Lord Jesus Christ, who has blessed us in Christ with every spiritual blessing in the heavenly places. (Ephesians 1:3)

Blessed be the God and Father of our Lord Jesus Christ! According to his great mercy, he has caused us to be born again to a living hope through the resurrection of Jesus Christ from the dead, to an inheritance that is imperishable, undefiled, and unfading, kept in heaven for you, who by God's power are being guarded through faith for a salvation ready to be revealed in the last time. (1 Peter 1:3–5)

Jesus said to them, "I am the bread of life; whoever comes to me shall not hunger, and whoever believes in me shall never thirst." (John 6:35)

Two problems that get in the way of everything: I make myself too big, and I make God too small.

Overcoming starts with reminding myself over and over that I seem wired to see the universe in this way: me in the center and God in the periphery. Just as David in Psalm 103 reminded his soul of the benefits of a life in God, I need to continually remind myself that I'm little and God is big.

I know it sounds simplistic, but in a way it really is simple.

And in a way, it's the hardest thing we'll ever do.

But winning starts with recognition of the problem.

When I come into his presence, I need to come acknowledging my wretchedness and the amazing banquet of his provision.

But I look away from the table, and I forget. Again and again.

And again and again, he nudges me to remember. There is a fountain of living water available to quench my thirst. Everything else I do to find satisfaction is a broken cistern.

11

DOWN, BUT NOT OUT

*Domesticating Jesus by
Hiding Our Sin*

WHILE SALLY SAT in Sunday morning worship listening with one ear to the sermon and with one ear to her own heart, another voice sought recognition. The Holy Spirit whispered about his love and her sin, about restoration and forgiveness.

But Sally just cringed and wrapped herself in a cloak of I'll-do-better-so-I-can-be-acceptable.

She glanced at Bob. Did God want her to tell him?

A Lesson from my Maasai Patient

To the Maasai, cows are everything.

Prestige. Wealth. The ability to buy more wives.

That's why when a thief snuck into Kanai Ole's boma, he didn't come for money. He came for cattle.

129

Kanai was used to guarding his father's cows. It was the way of their tribe. At night they gathered the animals into the center of their small compound surrounded by a thornbush fence for protection. During the day, vigilance was necessary as lion and leopard prowled to pick off stragglers that had wandered from the safety of the herd.

That day Kanai heard his father's cry. *Was it another lion attack?*

He ran toward his father's voice, but what he saw wasn't lion or leopard. It was a cattle rustler, with a knife held above his father, ready to strike.

Kanai lunged forward, intercepting the blow. He struck back, striking his fist against the thief. Kanai screamed to alert his neighbors as the thief ran across the dusty African plain.

He felt something wet on his chest. He placed his fingers on his neck. Something wasn't right. His neck bulged beneath his touch. His finger fell quickly into a laceration.

He felt a hand on his shoulder. "Kanai!"

His father's eyes widened with fear.

Kanai stumbled and fell to the earth, with blood now fountaining from his neck wound.

His father slipped the blanket off his own shoulders and pressed it against his son's neck.

Kanai could see the terror in his father's face. They were many kilometers from the main road and had no vehicle for transportation. He strained his eyes toward the horizon on the edge of the Rift Valley. High on the escarpment, he knew of a hospital.

But I will bleed to death before I ever get to the road.

Extend my metaphor comparing oxygen debt with gospel debt, and hemorrhage represents failure.

130

In this life, we all bleed. And concerning our faith, we all stumble. We're sinners. Sinners in need of grace.

So we all need to learn to deal with failure. We need to do it in a way that reflects the bigness of God's gospel plan and not default to a domesticated, weak Jesus who accepts us only once we've shown appropriate penitence.

Sooner rather than later.

When our bodies experience oxygen debt, the compensatory responses are immediate. Our bodies are demanding payment, and the currency is oxygen.

I experience this every time I walk up the series of steps leading from the hospital toward my son's school. My heart beats faster. My breathing quickens. Instantly.

Unfortunately, when we fall into gospel debt, some of our responses worsen rather than compensate our condition. Getting out of gospel debt has to begin with realizing it exists and is followed (if we want out) by conscious effort. It's not automatic.

We fail. It's going to happen. Remember what the apostle John said? "My little children, I am writing these things to you so that you may not sin. But if anyone does sin, we have an advocate with the Father, Jesus Christ the righteous" (1 John 2:1). Some versions say, "*And* if anyone does sin," not "*But*." I like that because it makes us understand that it's not the exception, it's the rule.

So what is our tendency when we fail?

We either gloss over it (*It's not that bad, it's only a white lie*), or we downright cover it up. We make excuses. We justify ourselves in our own eyes and in the eyes of others. Unfortunately, either tendency is only another manifestation of gospel debt. The other possibility is that we spend time wallowing in guilt.

I can easily remember Wally. He was my patient during the first month of my internship. I've forgotten every other patient that I cared for during that first month when I unleashed my fresh medical degree on the public, but Wally I'll never forget. His story was only part of the reason. He'd discovered his wife in an intimate encounter with another man. So he shot his wife and the other man before turning the gun on himself. He put the barrel of the gun in his mouth but tilted his hand a little too much, so that when he discharged the gun, he didn't die; he only blew off the front of his face.

By the time I arrived on the plastic surgery service at the Veterans Administration Hospital, Wally had already been a patient for eighteen months! Surgery after surgery had been performed to reconstruct the missing parts of his face. About once a week our team would go by and inject sterile water into stretchy tissue expanders located under his scalp. We were slowly stretching the skin of his scalp so it could be moved around to help create a nose and lips.

He was the kind of guy who would never look normal, and if your eyes met his in a gaze, I can nearly guarantee that you'd be the first to look away. Why? Because we want to avoid the shame associated with disfigurement.

Sometimes that's our tendency when we fail. We sin, but we don't really want to face it because of the shame.

The Bible encourages a direct approach to sin.

First of all, don't buy Satan's lies about you being the only one to be in that situation. *You thought what? You must really be weird.* We are all made of the same stuff. The longer I've been a physician, the more I think I've heard it all. Nothing surprises me anymore. So don't fall for the condemnation that the devil intends to pile on. Everyone is wired the same way. There's truth in the phrase, "but by the grace of God, there go I." The Bible says even a good man falls: "The righteous falls seven times and rises again" (Proverbs 24:16).

The initial step in approaching sin brings us right into the first step of the ABCs of spiritual resuscitation. Instead of covering it up or hiding behind a fig leaf, I need to face my sin head-on and confess I have a need.

"Whoever conceals his transgressions will not prosper; but he who confesses and forsakes them will obtain mercy" (Proverbs 28:13). According to my Microsoft Office 2004 dictionary, *forsake* means to abandon. Leave it alone. Don't keep it company anymore.

The way some of us act, you might think the Scripture said, "Confess and coddle." But it doesn't. We are to take our eyes off of our failure and put them back on Christ. Remember that Hebrews 12:1–3 says we are to lay aside the sin that clings and put our eyes on Christ.

There are few positive feedback loops in place in our physical bodies. One such positive feedback loop is commonly known as a death spiral. Here's how it works. The heart begins to fail, causing a decrease in the heart's output. Unfortunately, when output is down, that means that less oxygen is delivered to needy muscles, including the heart muscle itself. This causes the heart to fail further, lowering output, lessening oxygen delivery, and round and round it goes. In the rather crude lingo used by medical residents, we say a patient is "circling the drain." That implies that someone has already flushed, and it's only a matter of time.

Unfortunately, unless we intervene with the ABCs, often one failure (indicative of gospel debt) leads to a deepening of gospel debt as we try to excuse our sin or cover it up. It becomes a death spiral of sorts, one that can be stopped if we just step back and say, "I blew it."

Look at Joshua 7. After the children of Israel were defeated at Ai, the people fell on their faces. What did God say? "Get up!" (v. 10).

You're getting used to step B and C. Here are some key verses to help treat the gospel debt and nudge your soul into grace saturation.

> I acknowledged my sin to you,
>   and I did not cover my iniquity;
> I said, "I will confess my transgressions to the Lord,"
>   and you forgave the iniquity of my sin. (Psalm 32:5)

> For I am sure that neither death nor life, nor angels nor rulers, nor things present nor things to come, nor powers, nor height nor depth, nor anything else in all creation, will be able to separate us from the love of God in Christ Jesus our Lord. (Romans 8:38–39)

> If we confess our sins, he is faithful and just to forgive us our sins and to cleanse us from all unrighteousness. (1 John 1:9)

> In him we have redemption through his blood, the forgiveness of our trespasses, according to the riches of his grace. (Ephesians 1:7)

> The steps of a man are established by the Lord,
>   when he delights in his way;
> though he fall, he shall not be cast headlong,
>   for the Lord upholds his hand. (Psalm 37:23–24)

> I am writing you, little children, because your sins are forgiven for his name's sake. (1 John 2:12)

> For we do not have a high priest who is unable to sympathize with our weaknesses, but one who in every respect has been tempted as we are, yet without sin. Let us then with confidence draw near to the throne of grace, that we

may receive mercy and find grace to help in time of need. (Hebrews 4:15–16)

So you blew it. Confess. Forsake. Don't make it worse by covering it up or nursing yourself with condemnation. Get back on the horse. Get your eyes off the rulebook or you'll end up falling again. Remember, it's only by grace that we stand at all. When we realize we're weak, Christ's strength can shine.

As we learn to embrace these principles, we find ourselves dwelling more and more in a life saturated by grace: the knowledge that his love is given *in spite of* my weakness and sin. This is the life described by Paul in 2 Corinthians when he says that "the love of Christ controls us" (5:14). When our lives are dominated by the law, the rulebook is in constant focus, and we strive to improve ourselves. (This is tantamount to the raise-yourself-by-your-own-bootstraps philosophy.) From this position, when we fall, we easily find ourselves making excuses or falling headlong into self-pity and guilt. Conversely, if we have made grace our dwelling place, a fall from that position will not be the end! We only need to run to the gospel promises that will usher us quickly back into grace saturation.

Kanai Ole was carried into Kijabe Hospital, having survived miles of dirt roads while his friend kept a cloth pressed against his neck wound.

We transported him immediately to surgery, never removing pressure from his wound. Once in the operating room, Kanai was put under anesthesia. and his neck was prepped and sterile drapes applied in a square around his wound. Only when I had extended the neck wound to expose the blood vessels in the neck did we dare to remove the finger holding back the bleeding.

His jugular vein had been severed; the knife missed his carotid artery by only a few millimeters. After several minutes, the bleeding was stopped by tying off the cut ends of the jugular vein.

If we look at our metaphor to understand that we need to live a life in constant grace or gospel saturation, just as we need constant oxygen saturation, we can understand failure as a hemorrhage of sorts. The channels delivering the life-giving message of grace are temporarily severed.

The answer? Run to the cross, and glory in its sufficiency to place you in right standing before your Father. I domesticate Jesus every time I consider his cross to be inadequate to provide everything I need to make me perfect in God's presence.

Hemorrhage need not lead to fatality if a few basic principles are followed. Likewise, failures in our lives should be dealt with swiftly to minimize the amount of time we spend in gospel debt and get us back to a life characterized by God's love and grace.

12

GRACE IS THE KEY TO OVERCOMING NAGGING ADDICTIONS

Domesticating Jesus by Walking in Our Own Strength

DURING THE NEXT few weeks, Bob Christian watched Sally trudge forward through radiation therapy. Every time he saw the paleness of her skin or watched her walk breathlessly to the house from the mailbox, he fought a rising tide of panic.

And more and more he turned to a common social lubricant for help. *It's just a martini before dinner. Or two. I've got it under control.*

Cocktails before dinner. A shot before bed. *It will help me sleep.* Two or three beers during a football game. *You have to drink beer with pizza. Everyone does.*

Then there was the flask in his desk at work.

And another in his car.

For a while after college, he'd sworn off alcohol altogether. Then, after the kids were born, he didn't want to be a bad example. But as they grew, he thought it would be better if they were exposed to alcohol at home first, rather than find out about it at parties.

He felt guilty, but he couldn't quite seem to stay away. *I'm not as bad as my partner. It's not like it's affecting my work . . . or my family.*

Drink in hand, he looked into Sally's eyes. She shook her head. "Bob, what's going on?"

He turned away. "Don't judge me." He cleared his throat. "It helps me relax. I'll stop after you finish your therapy."

A salesclerk huddles against the building, enduring subfreezing temperature to smoke a cigarette.

Margie reaches for another handful of M&Ms, even though she isn't hungry.

Steve erases the history of the Internet sites he's visited that day at work, hoping desperately that no one will see where he's been.

A lonely mother pours another drink.

I Googled *addictions* and found references to just about anything and everything. Chocolate. Sex. The Internet. Instant messaging. E-mail. Masturbation. Food. Shopping. Chai. Exercise. Gossip. Television. World of Warcraft. Halo. Novels. Pornography. Sexual fantasies. Drugs (uppers, downers, even laxatives make the list). Motorcycles. Cars. Collections.

OK, I can see that I'm stepping on some toes here. And I can hear the excuses. "Hey, jogging isn't like pornography."

I understand that.

I'm referring to behaviors that are disruptive to our peace. Habits we perform, even to our hurt. We do them over and over, confessing our inability to control our appetites for the pleasure they bring us. Addictions are characterized by a lack of self-control.

I know that some addictions are psychologically and physiologically very complex. And I'm certainly not wanting to simplify the pain associated with drug, alcohol, and nicotine addiction; so for the most part, I'm not going to discuss them. If you want a raw look at what the hell of drug and alcohol addiction is all about (regardless of the authenticity of the author's account), read James Frey's *A Million Little Pieces*. And prepare to be shocked.

In this chapter I don't want to downplay that kind of addiction and the pain associated with it.

What I want to discuss is the nagging, sometimes daily behaviors that we can't seem to overcome. I want to be clear and call a spade a spade: we're talking about sin here. Some of the principles certainly apply to drug addictions, but again, because of the complexity of those problems and the physiological changes involved, I'm going to leave them out of formal discussion.

Let's address other problem areas. Imagine a man who just can't seem to stop viewing pornographic images on the Internet. It's not hard to see that this is sinful behavior as the viewing is always associated with lustful fantasies. Nonetheless, many men hide behind the "it's not hurting anyone" argument and fail to see their activity as the sin that it is. These people (women are included here, in growing numbers), because they don't see their need, won't move toward getting help. They will never begin the process of the ABCs, as the first step is an acknowledgment of their need. Until the blinders are off, they won't go for help.

So I'm not talking to them. I'm talking to those of you who are sickened by your habitual sin (whether porn, gossip, overeating, lying, petty thievery, cheating, or whatever) but just can't seem to win.

Put it in the light of our overall theme. Addictive behaviors make Jesus look small and domesticated. We've uninvited him from an area of struggle. We haven't admitted our smallness or his bigness (his adequacy to help).

You know the cycle, because we've all been there at some point in our lives. Sin. Confess. Maybe cry. Promise to do better. Sin. Confess. Do OK for a few days until something happens. It may be as small as our feelings being hurt and we turn to our addiction for comfort. Over and over we follow the cycle around, seemingly never able to pull ourselves free and feeling guilty every time we fall. Again and again and again.

The first step is in seeing your addiction for what it is: sin. John Piper has defined sin, in his book *Future Grace*, as anything we do to seek satisfaction outside of Christ. The addiction holds out a false promise of pleasure, and we sin when we believe the lie.

When I first read Piper's words, I was struck. How could someone as powerful, wonderful, gracious, and loving as Jesus not satisfy? How crazy is it that I regularly seek satisfaction outside of my relationship with Christ?

But seeing our addiction as sin does little but add shame and guilt to our problem. What we need is the ability to overcome.

But most of us are fighting the wrong way.

The writer of the book of Hebrews calls these problems "sin which clings so closely" (12:1). That's a wonderful description. Just when you think you have the problem licked, there it is again, clinging on behind you.

So we try harder. We promise we won't do it again. We make a vow. We gather up all the willpower and determination we can and season it with the power of positive thinking or some such psych. And then we fall again.

140

Paul gives us a hint as to how victory will be won against these nagging sins: "But I say, walk by the Spirit, and you will not gratify the desires of the flesh" (Galatians 5:16). Oh great, another phrase that we've spiritualized until no one seems sure what Paul was talking about. What is walking by the Spirit? We envision a holy man of sorts, eyes fixed on the clouds, walking in a zombie-like trance.

I think Paul meant something much more practical. Within the context of the whole book, Paul is talking about walking in grace. He's telling us that in order to win the battle over the flesh, we can't do it by the law. We have to do it by grace! "Are you so foolish? Having begun by the Spirit, are you now being perfected by the flesh?" (Galatians 3:3)

Let's go back and review a basic concept. How were we saved? By grace, right?

So right at salvation a huge victory was won over our sins, and it had *nothing* to do with us. It had everything to do with the cross, with who God is and what he does. Grace is the avenue. Grace is the divine quality whereby God freely loves, forgives, and exalts sinners into sonship. Grace frames every interaction that God has with his children. We were saved by grace, and by grace God moves us on toward the image of his son. "For those whom he foreknew he also predestined to be conformed to the image of his Son" (Romans 8:29).

Most of us have accepted the part of salvation by grace, but we've left the altar and decided to carry on in our own strength. We fail and feel guilty, and so we're reluctant to approach God for help. That's why addictions are so difficult to combat. Not only do we try to fight them in our own strength, we shrink away from grace because of our guilt.

Paul taught that we were crucified with Christ so that we could find freedom from our enslavement to sin.

Some of you are thinking, *That's exactly what my addiction is like. I'm a slave. It says jump and I ask, "How high?"*

So just what does being crucified with Christ mean? First, Paul says we "know" this to be true. That's something that the Holy Spirit settles in our hearts. "We know that our old self was crucified with him in order that the body of sin might be brought to nothing, so that we would no longer be enslaved to sin" (Romans 6:6).

A few verses later, Paul says we must "consider" this so. This is what the King James Version refers to as "reckoning": "So you also must consider yourselves dead to sin and alive to God in Christ Jesus" (Romans 6:11).

Paul speaks of being put to death with Christ so we will understand personally that a debt has been paid on our behalf. Christ died for our sins. In effect, we died, because that was what was required to pay off our debt. But Paul's metaphor of dying works on another level. We've died to the law, our marriage partner; so in effect we are out of its stranglehold on our souls and are now free to marry another, Christ, the personification of grace.

So walking in the Spirit and being crucified with Christ are both equated in the Scripture to overcoming enslavement to sin.

But what does it mean?

I believe the answer comes as we begin to experience the freedom of grace. "For sin will have no dominion over you, since you are not under law but under grace" (Romans 6:14). This is the secret to overcoming addiction: grace.

Paul makes it clear through Romans 6 and 7 that the law is powerless to help us live the life we desire. Concentrating on the law only seems to stimulate a desire within us to break the law. So in my efforts to win over addiction (habitual sin), by holding up my determination not to break the law . . . I fall.

In reading Romans 8, we gain more insight into just what Paul means by walking according to the Spirit. He says,

> For those who live according to the flesh set their minds on the things of the flesh, but those who live according to the Spirit set their minds on the things of the Spirit. For to set the mind on the flesh is death, but to set the mind on the Spirit is life and peace. (Romans 8:5–6)

It all works together. Considering ourselves dead and setting our mind on the things of the Spirit assist us in our fight for freedom.

If we keep our minds fixed on beating the problem (fulfilling the law), we fail. If we fix our minds on Christ, we find the victory we seek. Remember the sins that cling so closely? The writer of the book of Hebrews gives the same advice to win over clingy sins (addictions):

> Therefore, since we are surrounded by so great a cloud of witnesses, let us also lay aside every weight, and sin which clings so closely, and let us run with endurance the race that is set before us, looking to Jesus, the founder and perfecter of our faith, who for the joy that was set before him endured the cross, despising the shame, and is seated at the right hand of the throne of God. (Hebrews 12:1–2)

Paul links the two (setting our mind on Christ and being crucified) when he states,

> Set your minds on things that are above, not on things that are on earth. For you have died, and your life is hidden with Christ in God. (Colossians 3:2–3)

In the book of Galatians, Paul rebukes the believers for trying to complete by the law that which was begun by the Spirit (by grace). I love the way Eugene Petersen says it in his paraphrase *The Message.*

> You crazy Galatians! Did someone put a hex on you? Have you taken leave of your senses? Something crazy has happened, for it's obvious that you no longer have the crucified Jesus in clear focus in your lives. His sacrifice on the cross was certainly set before you clearly enough.
>
> Let me put this question to you: How did your new life begin? Was it by working your heads off to please God? Or was it by responding to God's Message to you? Are you going to continue this craziness? For only crazy people would think they could complete by their own efforts what was begun by God. If you weren't smart enough or strong enough to begin it, how do you suppose you could perfect it? (Galatians 3:1–3)

An answer to our sin dilemma is coming into focus. We can't beat this by determining to keep the law. Winning comes when we begin to accept the gospel of grace as powerful and adequate enough to keep us from sin.

Perhaps contrasting the two methods will help us understand how walking in grace (walking in the Spirit) works:

If I battle according to the flesh, I concentrate on the law. If I battle according to the Spirit, I concentrate on grace. In the flesh, the emphasis is on me conquering sin. In the Spirit, the emphasis is on Christ in me conquering sin. In the flesh, I work. In the Spirit, God works. In the flesh, sin is central. In the Spirit, the cross is central. In the flesh, I'm seeking justification by works. In the Spirit, I accept the work of the cross as sufficient, a work of grace. In the flesh, I concentrate on me. In the Spirit, my eyes are on Christ.

Have you ever tried to not think a thought? The very act of not trying to think of something forces you to fail! This is a big part of the problem in trying not to sin. The very act of trying not to sin places sin in focus, and we are ensnared by the temptation.

So do I just ignore sin?

Not exactly. Walking in the Spirit isn't passive. It's active with the focus on the cross. And guess what happens when my thoughts are set on the things of the Spirit? Gratitude. Wonder. Jesus and his cross grow.

The good news about concentrating on Christ is that as he becomes my focus, my desire for sin falls away. I've beaten the addiction not by sheer strength of my will but by falling in love with Jesus. "Delight yourself in the Lord, and he will give you the desires of your heart" (Psalm 37:4).

Prosperity doctrine teaches us (wrongly) that God will give us what we desire, but that's not what this verse says, is it? It says he will give us *the desires*.

When I'm keeping grace in focus, I naturally begin to pour this grace onto others around me.

I believe understanding how much God loves us and walking in the freshness of that knowledge gives us an idea about what walking in the Spirit is all about. The knowledge of his love for us is to be the controlling passion of our lives. It's all tied into the concept of being dead to sin. Look at what Paul teaches:

> For the love of Christ controls us, because we have concluded this: that one has died for all, therefore all have died; and he died for all, that those who live might no longer live for themselves but for him who for their sake died and was raised. (2 Corinthians 5:14–15)

He loves me. Loves me! As that knowledge begins to penetrate my soul, my need for the law falls away. His grace teaches me about holiness, and I die to the law. That's what walking in the Spirit is all about.

An ironic key to winning over addiction is not knowing how strong I am, but knowing how desperately weak I am. So weak that I can never stop on my own. But it's when I'm weak that grace can work through me. God rarely works in an area where I feel self-sufficient. Christ works when I've given up.

> For through the law I died to the law, so that I might live to God. I have been crucified with Christ. It is no longer I who live, but Christ who lives in me. And the life I now live in the flesh I live by faith in the Son of God, who loved me and gave himself for me. (Galatians 2:19–20)

Much of the battle against habitual sin in our lives is fought in the mind. It is in our thoughts that we consider ourselves dead to sin. We set our focus on the things of the Spirit, on grace, and begin to see our behavior change positively as we focus on him. "And we all, with unveiled face, beholding the glory of the Lord, are being transformed into the same image from one degree of glory to another. For this comes from the Lord who is the Spirit" (2 Corinthians 3:18). Notice when the change comes. When we are beholding the glory of the Lord.

When I try not to do something, I fail.

Winning over Sin

The sad truth is that many Christians today have remained infants in their understanding of how to win the battle over sin.

They have accepted salvation by grace but walk forward fighting against sin as if they have to do it on their own. Week after week they hear messages from the pulpit that reinforce the pick-me-up-by-the-bootstraps mentality. Pray more. Witness more. Get more disciplined about growth.

So they limp along, trying and failing, feeling guilty, then falling into the trap of some comforting sinful behavior to ease their guilt. *I'll just fall again. I might as well give up.*

That would be a wonderful place to start.

We have failed a generation of American Christians who have embraced a self-made-man concept of faith. We have allowed a strong work ethic to poison our faith. Christians who worship at the altar of humanism are destined to a life of struggle with the mud of sin constantly clinging to their boots.

What Sunday school teacher wouldn't be proud of students who proclaimed that they were going to work harder, pray harder, and make every effort not to fall into sin? Alas, John Wayne, not Jesus, has become our Lord.

It is God's job to work. Our job is to rest.

Paul would be exasperated with our pitiful attempts to be perfect by our own efforts. What would his letter look like to us? "Oh foolish Americans, who has bewitched you?"

We don't need to pray more, witness more, and memorize more. God asks us to set our minds on him. In essence, to love him more.

Walking in the Spirit doesn't have to remain weird and super-spiritual. It is centered in relationship and the knowledge that the Spirit of God is indwelling us as a result of the cross.

We need to stop focusing on our sin and focus on the One who died to bury our sin in the sea of forgetfulness. And in focusing on him, we find the desires for sin becoming less and our desire to love him growing.

I can imagine that some of you are reading these words and thinking, *It can't be that easy.*

But it is. Dear brother or sister, meditate on the passages I've quoted. Victory is ours if we only give up and realize that our strength is immaterial. It is Christ in us who wins over sin, and he gets the glory in the process. We began by grace, and by grace we will be victorious over sin. For some of us who have been discouraged by our inability to win over sin, this is nothing short of the most liberating news of all. Go forward in grace, just as it was by grace you have been saved.

For some of you, the pattern of fail, repent, promise to do better, fail, and repent has become a way of life, pushing you toward the precipice of hopelessness. Let this realization of your inability be the starting point. We can't be victorious. But Christ in us can.

We cannot keep temptation from occurring. This can be a stumbling block, especially to Christians whose habitual sin is in the area of lust. We lose if we equate the temptation with failure. A passing thought can come from anywhere, even our enemy. Satan whispers his lies, and if we equate a thought with failure, we fall. Discouragement and guilt compound our situation. A fleeting thought does not constitute a failure and should not prompt immediate introspection and analysis. This only causes us to focus on the unwanted intrusion and the likelihood that a passing thought becomes a dwelling spot for our thoughts progressing to desire and fantasy.

My advice on such issues is to let such thoughts pass without giving them the honor of analysis. Let the first disturbing thought prod you into the arms of Christ and an acknowledgment of your need. Helpless is where we begin. Run to the ABCs!

A life of peace, where God's love has saturated our hearts, a life of walking in the Spirit, beckons. Find yourself weak enough to embrace it!

Spiritual Resuscitation

Let's look one more time at the emergency evaluation of someone mired in habitual sin.

Often there's a problem with **A**, acknowledging your need. Most of our failures with habitual sins come because we are relying on our own strength. It is only when we finally reach the end of our own efforts that we open ourselves to the strength of Christ. If we, in our pride, are still content to bear down with grit and determination and fight our sin nature on our own, we will lose, because we have not started down the path of soul resuscitation.

Once we've seen our need, latching onto the truth of the gospel and believing it will be the heart of the battle. We began by faith, recognizing that the cross of Christ completely bridges the gap between our wretchedness and God's perfection. So we now are to press forward in faith, living each moment in awareness that the same grace will teach us how to live.

Here is a focused list, a beginning point for finding a cure. Think of this not as a prescription to be finished in seven days but as a vitamin supplement needed daily. Ask God to make these verses alive in your experience. That will take care of **B**, believe, and **C**, communion.

Now it is evident that no one is justified before God by the law, for "The righteous shall live by faith." (Galatians 3:11)

But if you are led by the Spirit, you are not under the law. (Galatians 5:18)

But far be it from me to boast except in the cross of our Lord Jesus Christ, by which the world has been crucified to me, and I to the world. . . . And as for all who walk by this rule, peace and mercy be upon them, and upon the Israel of God. (Galatians 6:14, 16)

For sin will have no dominion over you, since you are not under law but under grace. (Romans 6:14)

For God has done what the law, weakened by the flesh, could not do. By sending his own Son in the likeness of sinful flesh and for sin, he condemned sin in the flesh, in order that the righteous requirement of the law might be fulfilled in us, who walk not according to the flesh but according to the Spirit. (Romans 8:3–4)

For everyone who has been born of God overcomes the world. And this is the victory that has overcome the world—our faith. Who is it that overcomes the world except the one who believes that Jesus is the Son of God? (1 John 5:4–5)

No temptation has overtaken you that is not common to man. God is faithful, and he will not let you be tempted beyond your ability, but with the temptation he will also provide the way of escape, that you may be able to endure it. (1 Corinthians 10:13)

Commit your way to the Lord;
    trust in him, and he will act.
He will bring forth your righteousness as the light,
    and your justice as the noonday. (Psalm 37:5–6)

It is God's job to bring forth our righteousness and our job to trust.

For the grace of God has appeared, bringing salvation for all people, training us to renounce ungodliness and worldly passions, and to live self-controlled, upright, and godly lives in the present age, waiting for our blessed hope, the appearing of the glory of our great God and Savior Jesus Christ, who gave himself for us to redeem us from all lawlessness and to purify for himself a people for his own possession who are zealous for good works. (Titus 2:11–14)

Notice that it is a work of grace, not the law, that trains us to live with self-control.

For one who has died has been set free from sin. (Romans 6:7)

So Jesus said to the Jews who had believed in him, "If you abide in my word, you are truly my disciples, and you will know the truth, and the truth will set you free." (John 8:31–32)

For freedom Christ has set us free; stand firm therefore, and do not submit again to a yoke of slavery. (Galatians 5:1)

13

THE GOSPEL OF THE DOMESTICATED JESUS

It's Really All about Me, Isn't It?

WE'VE BEEN LOOKING at some of the hundreds of small ways we domesticate Christ. Worry, guilt, fear, anxiety, sinful addictions. Let's shift for a moment and think about the real gospel and how very far away the gospel of a domesticated Jesus looks.

When we domesticate Jesus into a divine vending machine, the gospel begins to look very different.

The real gospel is start-to-finish about a work of God. He initiates hunger and awareness of sin. He calls and provides forgiveness through the work of Jesus at the cross. God is central, and he gets the attention and glory.

The gospel of a domesticated Jesus is all about me. My needs, my wants, my testimony, my ministry, my ability to do all the

153

THE GOSPEL OF THE DOMESTICATED JESUS

"Christian" stuff. It's all about me. Oh, I'm thankful all right. Thankful that God has used me to do good works. Thankful that he has given me a wonderful testimony to serve as an example to so many who admire me.

When Jesus assumes his rightful place, prayer is all about aligning my will with his. It is characterized by thankfulness and awe. I submit my wants and my desires to him and *listen*.

Prayer for those of us accustomed to domesticating Jesus takes on a different role. It's all about me, remember. Prayer sounds more like advice than submission and awe. *You know, God, you really need to change the way my wife thinks.* Prayer isn't about aligning my will with his. The domesticated Jesus aligns his will with mine. I name it and claim it. I really need a new car, a new house, a new TV. Of course, I'll use it for ministry. My needs, not Jesus, are central. Prayer in the name of a domesticated Jesus is all about *talking*, not listening.

We domesticate Jesus every time we try to make him fit our agenda instead of listening to his.

Domesticating an animal usually involves fences.

Domesticating Christ does too.

Fences? Sure. For example, the time-fence. Jesus is domesticated by slotting him into one hour on Sunday morning rather than recognizing my *continuous* need.

How about the I'll-serve-him-as-long-as-it's-convenient fence? How about the as-long-as-I'm-comfortable-fence? We're happy to serve as long as it doesn't impact our free time or our wallets.

Certainly Jesus didn't really mean all of that stuff he said about sacrifice, persecution, and suffering, did he?

Sure he did. He promised that tribulation and persecution would come.

I have said these things to you, that in me you may have peace. In the world you will have tribulation. But take heart; I have overcome the world. (John 16:33)

For to this you have been called, because Christ also suffered for you, leaving you an example, so that you might follow in his steps. (1 Peter 2:21)

For it has been granted to you that for the sake of Christ you should not only believe in him but also suffer for his sake. (Philippians 1:29)

But that's not the way it works in vending-machine Christianity.

In the gospel of a domesticated Christ, the cross loses power. His agony is denied. The cross is gilded. A decoration. A necklace rather than an instrument of torture and death.

The gospel of the domesticated Christ is all about saving me. Even saving others takes a backseat.

How so?

One domesticated Christ is soft, unwilling to damn anyone. Another holds out a palm branch to all the other world religions, offering one more way to find God.

The real, sovereign Christ makes a bold claim. "No one comes to the Father except through me" (John 14:6).

A domesticated light of the world is a wimpy candle. The light of the real Jesus is more akin to the brightest star giving off the power of thousands of nuclear explosions every second.

Even if we believe Jesus is the only way and is willing to damn unbelievers, we domesticate him when we fail to share the good news so as not to offend or inconvenience others. (Or are we just concerned about our own image, not wanting to be perceived as radical or weird?)

Just how offended and inconvenienced will they be when they are screaming in the fires of hell?

A popular view of Jesus is a particularly disturbing one to me. It's the prosperity-domesticated one that places my needs and wants front and center. It's not just the name-it-and-claim-it version or the give-so-you-will-be-blessed one. A more subtle version has infiltrated the western church and denies sacrifice and suffering as part of the normative Christian experience.

At the core, greed has gained a handhold in this version of Christianity. For that reason, I want to look a bit more closely at this dangerous symptom.

Greed

Working in a rural hospital in Kenya, I frequently have days like I had today.

Days when I just shake my western head in wonder over a clinical situation. *Why do my patients wait so long before seeking help?*

My patient, a forty-four-year-old woman, came with a huge ulcerative mass growing in her right breast. Bleeding. Oozing. And smelling much less than fresh.

I've seen this type of neglect over and over, enough that, although it is still heartbreaking, I think I've begun to understand. There is no money for treatment. She's probably been seen in a rural clinic that did what she could afford: dressing changes a few times a week. Or worse, she's probably been seeing a "traditional healer," basically a witch doctor who fed her some herbs or burned her skin with a glowing fire-stick. By the time this particular patient came to my clinic, she'd been putting up with the cancer for eight months.

From natural history studies we understand that it had likely been hiding deep in the breast for years, dividing and growing unnoticed. By the time a cancer is one centimeter in diameter, it has probably been growing for six years.

Six years?

That's the disturbing truth. Imagine a single cell deep within the breast that starts to deviate from the normal rules of growth and social behavior. We call the transformation into cancer a mutation. The normal doubling time for breast cancer is anywhere from two to four months. So for now it's only one cancer cell hiding happily in the midst of normal neighbors. In two months or so, it has become two; a few months after that, it's four cells. You see? It takes a long time before it's even palpable or able to be felt by the human finger.

My patient looked thin, a contrast to her greedy cancer that had snarfed up all the nutrition it could get.

I'm sure by now you see where I'm taking this metaphor, and while I'm sorry if some of you are offended by descriptions of malodorous, oozing tumors, I think the bigger offense is made by the cancerous attitude of greed that threatens to leave us spiritually malnourished.

Greed, like cancer, often lurks unseen, beneath the surface, lingering for some time before becoming symptomatic. And like cancer, once fully apparent, it tends to drain life from other more functional areas of life.

Greed isn't just about money. It's about my time, my possessions, and the things that are precious to me, including my home as well as the talents God has given me.

It can be as simple and hidden as the absence of generosity. Instead of having joy, we find our hearts resentful and cold toward those in need. No one else knows. But we know. And as it grows, our view of our gifts and possessions makes a subtle change.

As I consider yet another request for help or money, a few things give me perspective. Foremost is the fact that I am only a steward. That goes for talents, family, and spiritual fruit as well as material possessions. *It's all God's!* "Every good gift and every perfect gift is from above, coming down from the Father of lights with whom there is no variation or shadow due to change" (James 1:17). It didn't start with me. I didn't earn it or deserve it.

I can hear some of you shifting in your seats. How do I know that makes you uncomfortable?

Because it bothers me too. We huff and pose. *I worked hard for this! Certainly it's my due!*

It helps me to realize that every breath I take is just one more reminder of God's grace, his undeserved favor.

It's well worth studying 2 Corinthians 8–9 to see an example of generosity that was held up for us to see. Check out the high points. The churches of Macedonia were praised because they gave from a position of need.

> For in a severe test of affliction, their abundance of joy and their extreme poverty have overflowed in a wealth of generosity on their part. (2 Corinthians 8:2)

Sounds a bit like another familiar account found in Mark.

> And a poor widow came and put in two small copper coins, which make a penny. And he [Jesus] called his disciples to him and said to them, "Truly, I say to you, this poor widow has put in more than all those who are contributing to the offering box. For they all contributed out of their abundance, but she out of her poverty has put in everything she had, all she had to live on." (Mark 12:42–44)

The Macedonians gave "beyond their means" (2 Corinthians 8:3) and "of their own free will" (v. 3, NLT). Jesus is seen as the ultimate example.

> For you know the grace of our Lord Jesus Christ, that though he was rich, yet for your sake he became poor, so that you by his poverty might become rich. (2 Corinthians 8:9)

There could be no end to giving, and I'm not saying we are obligated to give everything away. Paul cautioned the Corinthians,

> I do not mean that others should be eased and you burdened, but that as a matter of fairness your abundance at the present time should supply their need, so that their abundance may supply your need, that there may be fairness. (2 Corinthians 8:13–14)

It's an unfortunate trend that the top earners in American society give a lesser percent of their income, far below the 10-percent tithe bar set in the Scripture.

Oh, tithing is just another way that legalism creeps into your life.

It could be.

Or our unwillingness to consider giving a tenth of our income could just be another symptom of gospel debt. Or an example of how our lack of trust in God's provision domesticates Jesus. Again.

It could reflect ingratitude at being given so much at the price of the cross.

It could mean that we're seeking pleasure from material stuff, stuff that in the end can never satisfy like Jesus does.

Or our resistance to tithing could be the fact that we're so into grace that any suggestion of the law is revolting to us.

But I doubt it.

I believe the cure for greed is on the way when we make a conscious decision toward generosity. The cure is closer when we concentrate on the truth of the gospel until our hearts overflow with joy, and that in turn often results in an overflow of generosity. Remember, Paul explained that the Macedonians' joy overflowed in generosity.

Concentrate on the material blessings around us, and we'll lean toward closing our hands. Concentrate on the Giver of the material blessings, and we'll find our hands open, holding onto all our accumulated "stuff" loosely.

Take a moment to review the fallout we've seen from this great salvation. Instead of anxiety, we've been offered peace. Instead of anger, love. Instead of discontentment, satisfaction. Because of the gospel, we can exchange hope for discouragement. We learn to walk in the Spirit to overcome addictions to sin. We have victory and forgiveness instead of failure and bitterness. And now we are invited into a larger life, free of greed, a day-by-day reliance on God where we open ourselves to being channels of his love toward those around us. That means grace to the undeserving as well as our time, our money, and our lives are all on the altar of his agenda, not ours.

Again, we can't do it.

Do you recognize the recurrent theme? Sanctification is God's work. Our job is to trust, to adore. Our boast is in the cross.

And that brings us back to the ABC principles of soul resuscitation aimed at helping us to keep experiencing being "saved to the uttermost" (Hebrews 7:25).

A. Acknowledge your need. *Lord, I just can't seem to shed my old nature. I can't do it. But I so want to be like you, to live a life where everything I am and have is open to be used for your purposes.*

B. Believe the promises inherent in the gospel, and **C**, spend time in communion with these promises in quietness before God.

Cancer is treatable by multiple modalities, but almost all involve some personal suffering. Surgery, chemotherapy, and radiation can all be effective weapons in the fight, but all have the potential for negative side effects.

The treatment of greed may take repeated doses of the basics and a periodic spiritual chemotherapy of sorts. Remember, concentrate on the awesomeness of your Heavenly Father and on his love for you, a love that launched a nearly unbelievable plan for our rescue from hell.

Killing the root of greed means a strike against self, the idol of "I" where *my* needs, *my* desire for pleasure, and *my* wants are central.

Walking in the Spirit means dying to self. Refer back to the discussion on addictions for more assistance in unraveling the mystery of walking in the Spirit.

Rx

Giving is an area where God wants us to excel. We don't give to the deserving. That's not grace; it's wages. Giving is to be an "act of grace."

Here are a few verses (spiritual chemo) to fight the soul-cancer of greed:

> But as you excel in everything—in faith, in speech, in knowledge, in all earnestness, and in our love for you—see that you excel in this act of grace also. (2 Corinthians 8:7)

Giving is to come from the overflow of love that God has placed in our hearts (grace, walking in the Spirit, his life in me), not as a dutiful fulfillment of a command (law, walking in the flesh, our own strength). Remember, "For God so loved the world, that he gave . . ." (John 3:16).

> I say this not as a command, but to prove by the earnestness of others that your love also is genuine. (2 Corinthians 8:8)

> Each one must give as he has decided in his heart, not reluctantly or under compulsion, for God loves a cheerful giver. And God is able to make all grace abound to you, so that having all sufficiency in all things at all times, you may abound in every good work. (2 Corinthians 9:7–8)

Greed is about serving me. Generosity is about serving others.

> . . . the Son of Man came not to be served but to serve, and to give his life as a ransom for many. (Matthew 20:28)

> Let each of you look not only to his own interests, but also to the interests of others. Have this mind among yourselves, which is yours in Christ Jesus, who, though he was in the form of God, did not count equality with God a thing to be grasped, but made himself nothing, taking the form of a servant, being born in the likeness of men. And being found in human form, he humbled himself by becoming obedient to the point of death, even death on a cross. (Philippians 2:4–8)

> But God shows his love for us in that while we were still sinners, Christ died for us. (Romans 5:8)

> And walk in love, as Christ loved us and gave himself up for us, a fragrant offering and sacrifice to God. (Ephesians 5:2)

He who did not spare his own Son but gave him up for us all, how will he not also with him graciously give us all things? (Romans 8:32)

As for the rich in this present age, charge them not to be haughty, nor to set their hopes on the uncertainty of riches, but on God, who richly provides us with everything to enjoy. They are to do good, to be rich in good works, to be generous and ready to share, thus storing up treasure for themselves as a good foundation for the future, so that they may take hold of that which is truly life. (1 Timothy 6:17–19)

All of the daily "disasters" that we've talked about so far (anxiety, anger, guilt, greed, etc.) can be thought of as the fallout of a life lived in the service of self, a life lived in celebration of the gospel of a domesticated Christ. It is the "good life" where we are on the throne, material possessions promise to bring fulfillment, and our future is what we make it (i.e., the "American Dream"). What God is offering us in the gospel is nothing short of freedom from a dead life and a life of self-service, a life where love is the currency, peace is the result, and our boast is the cross.

This is what Paul tells Timothy is "truly life."

The gospel of the real Jesus is perfect. It's all about him. In the real gospel, I get to confess my greed and call it the sin that it is. The central focus of the gospel of the real Jesus is the cross. Sacrifice isn't something I do to gain acceptance. The cross already did that. Sacrifice and suffering can be the avenues God uses to help us find our treasure in him.

Yes, Christ promises us abundant life, but I'm not allowed to define the ins and outs of abundance. It doesn't mean I'll drive the fastest car, live in the nicest house, and have the best job. But it does mean that God is the one who is sovereign over all of these details in my life. Because of the cross, I can't claim a pain-free life, but I can know the grace that promises to sustain me no matter what the cost.

The abundance Jesus promises has to do with peace in the midst of turmoil, grace in the midst of pain. Confidence replaces fear, and hope dawns after the darkest of nights.

Because I hold the hand of the real Jesus, I don't need to be afraid of sacrifice and risk. If he's in control and I'm in hardship, then I believe he has allowed it for my good.

Because the real Jesus demands our all, the gospel will always stand juxtaposed against the American Dream. That means that the true gospel will never find itself in the "in" position in American culture.

Do my attitudes always conform to the gospel of the real Jesus?

Sadly, no.

But that's why I'm challenging myself (along with my readers) to dissect below the skin of our belief structure.

Let's make sure that Christ is at the center.

Characteristics of the Life Lived in Service of the Real Jesus

OK, so I've made it clear that I think we domesticate Christ when we treat him as if he exists to make our lives cozy and prosperous. So just what does a life lived in service of the real Jesus look like?

A Life of Love

When a physician is trying to make a diagnosis, certain characteristics, symptoms, or findings are said to be pathognomonic.

That is, when present, a diagnosis is positive. For example, I could say that finding mycobacterium tuberculosis bacteria on a slide of a patient's sputum is pathognomonic of pulmonary tuberculosis. On the other hand, right lower quadrant abdominal pain is not pathognomonic of appendicitis, because there are other diseases that can present with right lower quadrant pain.

When speaking of defining qualities of Christians, Jesus made it clear that there are certain earmarks of the Christian—qualities that define us. "By this all people will know that you are my disciples, if you have love for one another" (John 13:35). I believe that a life lived in pursuit of the real Jesus will result in this defining quality—love. If love isn't present at least some of the time, we have just cause to question the presence of real faith.

The essence of love is putting someone else's interests above our own. This is quite the antithesis to the popular prosperity gospel, where my needs come first.

A Life of Carrying the Cross

> And he said to all, "If anyone would come after me, let him deny himself and take up his cross daily and follow me." (Luke 9:23)

Typical to a belief in a prosperity gospel is the feeling that the cross exists only to solve the problem of my sin punishment. When the gospel is twisted in this way, the cross is only there to pave the way for my forgiveness and my entrance into heaven. Certainly it is completely adequate in that regard, but the cross also exists as an example of the lifestyle we are being asked to follow. The cross is to be lifted and carried by every Christian, not to purchase salvation, but as a way to bring more glory to our wonderful Savior. A life lived in denial of self (a life that is lived in such a way that people can see that Christ and not stuff is our real treasure) is a life that brings him glory.

The cross means sacrifice, not for the sake of merit, but for the sake of making Jesus look big.

The cross means others first and kingdom first. Carrying our cross means recognizing that I'm small and Jesus is big.

Doesn't sound like much fun at first glance.

That's why you have to take a long look. A life of risk, self-denial, and sacrifice is the path to an abundant, joy-filled life. We'll take a look at that in more detail in the chapter on gospel fallout.

A Life Lived in Saturation of Grace

Do I really understand the concept of grace saturation? A life lived in service of the real Jesus recognizes the abundance of grace that frames his every interaction with me. Every blessing that comes my way is undeserved, yet it is given freely because he loves me without condition. Sonship and all the benefits of being a child of a King are mine simply because of the cross and are due to no worth of my own.

So I don't have to strive to make him love me more. Sharing my faith and praying with patients doesn't mean God likes me better at the close of the day. Sure, he is pleased with me, but the works don't purchase his favor. Favor with God was purchased solely on the basis of Calvary's tree.

I find that for so many Christians, grace remains a nebulous concept, something akin to being gentle and kind. Real grace is so much more. Grace is a godly characteristic that determines his posture toward his children whereby he generously and freely loves, forgives, and exalts undeserving sinners into sonship.

166

Anytime I am behaving as if there is something I can do to earn or merit God's favor, I have fallen away from the gospel of the real Jesus, because the real Jesus is a God of grace.

I know there are other ways to describe a life lived in service to the real Jesus, but these are (or should be) near the top of your list of descriptors. Love. Sacrifice. Grace.

Could anything stop a church characterized by this triad?

A more troubling question for me is: *Do these characterize my life?*

14

WHEN HOPE FALTERS

Discouragement When Jesus Is Small

WEEKS GRINDED ON weeks as Sally's therapy continued and she fought to keep her head above a sea of discouragement. Bob had been supportive, but Sally worried that her husband's alcohol problem was increasing, and she felt unable to help. She felt tired *all the time*, and the regret in her soul was taking its toll.

It wasn't until a series of tests at the completion of her radiation therapy that Sally was able to close her hand around that elusive missing piece: hope.

Dr. Marcus O'Reilly smiled and set her file on his desk. "It's all good news, Sally. There's no evidence of cancer now. We still need to continue the monthly chemotherapy treatments, but right now it's all focused on reducing your chances of a possible recurrence."

A missionary loses heart after years in a difficult place without seeing any converts. A parent despairs over a teen making bad

169

choices. An office worker is overlooked for a pay raise after years of service. A Christian fights an addiction to Internet pornography, losing hope of gaining freedom.

We all face discouragement to varying degrees. No one can stay "up" all the time.

But prolonged discouragement should prompt us to draw away from the bustle of life and ask, as David did, "Why are you cast down, O my soul?" (Psalm 42:11).

Years ago, shortly after the publication of my first novel, *Stainless Steal Hearts*, I faced the temptation of discouragement. Novel writing isn't for the faint of soul. It takes days, weeks, and months to crank out a story, and for the beginner there's the inconvenience of fitting it in around another occupation. For me, like most novelists, I dreamed of big sales and interviews. But months after publication, with sales dribbling forward, self-pity took a seat beside me. *I worked so hard and this is all I see?*

Then the mail brought an unexpected joy, a letter from a reader. The note was from a librarian at a correctional facility who'd been asked to review my book for their library. She hadn't even wanted to read the book; she opened the cover because it was her job. She explained that she had seen herself in one of the characters, a young woman whose illicit affair was much like her own. She too had an affair with an older, powerful man and made moral compromises to keep him. *Just like my character.* What caught my attention was how the Holy Spirit clearly placed his finger on her conscience. The last name I had given to the powerful, older man was the same as the man with whom she'd had an affair: Redman.

God had a plan for my writing. And through the letter, I was reminded that I needed to rest in his agenda and his timing, not in mine.

What is the secret element that the letter helped restore? What is lacking in our lives when we face times of discouragement?

Hope.

Have you waited months or years for a loved one to come to Christ? Have you toiled without recognition? Have you fallen into the same trap over and over again? Do you have the sense that your prayers go no higher than the ceiling, that no one sees your chronic pain?

Cling fast to the hope that is ours by right. If there is anything that is ours by virtue of our salvation, it is hope. "Through him we have also obtained access by faith into this grace in which we stand, and we rejoice in hope of the glory of God" (Romans 5:2).

Almost any darkness can be endured if we trust that there will be light in the future. The despair of patients facing pain is often lifted if they know relief is available. Without hope, our hearts fail. "Hope deferred makes the heart sick, but a desire fulfilled is a tree of life" (Proverbs 13:12).

How did we come to Christ?

It was God's work, independent of our worthiness. And just as he was faithful in calling us to him, our future is in his hands.

Capable hands. Hands of a big God. "And I am sure of this, that he who began a good work in you will bring it to completion at the day of Jesus Christ" (Philippians 1:6).

If we are discouraged, is it because we have fashioned our Savior as a weak, inadequate conqueror? Is he inadequate to soothe the wounds of our souls? Has he been domesticated into a small and insignificant role insulting to the ruler of the universe?

If we start through our resuscitation priorities, we quickly assess **A**. Has discouragement prompted us to look outside of God (how ridiculous is this?) for a solution? (Have we *acknowledged*

171

our need?) There are times when our discouragement is borne of our own pride. If we have taken over God's job in securing our futures, we have the right to discouraging thoughts. If we are relying on our own merit to stand before God, we will soon tire of our inability. There is just no way that in our own strength (relying on the false gospel of pride) we can be good enough for long enough to deserve Heaven.

If we find no problem at **A**, we will certainly find it at **B**. If we have lost hope, we have failed to *believe* the truth of the gospel.

Pore over these verses, and ask God to awaken your soul to the truth. Acknowledge quickly that you are small and needy and that he is big and mighty.

Prescription for Discouragement—Rx: HOPE!

So when God desired to show more convincingly to the heirs of the promise the unchangeable character of his purpose, he guaranteed it with an oath, so that by two unchangeable things, in which it is impossible for God to lie, we who have fled for refuge *might have strong encouragement* to hold fast to the *hope* set before us. We have this as a *sure and steadfast anchor of the soul*, a *hope* that enters into the inner place behind the curtain, where Jesus has gone as a forerunner on our behalf, having become a high priest forever after the order of Melchizedek. (Hebrews 6:17–20)

Blessed be the God and Father of our Lord Jesus Christ! According to his great mercy, he has caused us to be born again to a living hope through the resurrection of Jesus Christ from the dead. (1 Peter 1:3)

For to this end we toil and strive, because we have our hope set on the living God, who is the Savior of all people, especially of those who believe. (1 Timothy 4:10)

For I know that my Redeemer lives,
and at the last he will stand upon the earth. (Job 19:25)

He delivered us from such a deadly peril, and he will deliver us. On him we have set our hope that he will deliver us again. (2 Corinthians 1:10)

For because he himself has suffered when tempted, he is able to help those who are being tempted. (Hebrews 2:18)

Are there any among the false gods of the nations that can
bring rain?
Or can the heavens give showers?
Are you not he, O Lord our God?
We set our hope on you,
for you do all these things. (Jeremiah 14:22)

Ask yourself, like Jeremiah the prophet, "Are there any among the false gospels that can offer hope?" Consider carefully the words of David. When he was discouraged, he talked to himself, urging his soul to hope!

Why are you cast down, O my soul,
and why are you in turmoil within me?
Hope in God; for I shall again praise him,
my salvation and my God. (Psalm 42:11; cf. v. 5)

For I know the plans I have for you, declares the Lord, plans for welfare and not for evil, to give you a future and a hope. (Jeremiah 29:11)

The Lord of hosts has sworn:
"As I have planned,
    so shall it be,
and as I have purposed,
    so shall it stand." (Isaiah 14:24)

Remind your soul of the greatness of our Savior. Is not our discouragement another symptom that we have refashioned an inadequate reflection of Jesus?

15

SHORT-CIRCUITING THE FLOW OF GRACE

Domesticating Jesus by Our Bitterness

THE FIRST TIME I saw Ibrahim Mohamed in my surgery clinic in Kijabe, Kenya, he looked six months pregnant.

But men don't get pregnant.

He came, like so many of our Somali patients, as a casualty of war. He wasn't a soldier, just another innocent bystander caught in the wrong place at the wrong time. Several years before, he had been the victim of a shrapnel injury to his left leg just below the crease where his leg joined the abdomen.

But he didn't come to me because of his leg. He came because his abdomen had begun to swell.

Just sitting there on the exam table, I could see the visible swelling rising up out of the pelvis and poking through his clothes. Especially where there is a language barrier, the physician is tempted to skip the history and launch straight into the physical exam looking for clues.

175

But that's not the way it should be done.

So I asked questions and listened through my interpreter. Ibrahim had a story, one that would provide the clues to his present dilemma.

He had been treated for the shrapnel injury in Mogadishu. It didn't seem like that big of a deal.

Until his leg began to buzz. Ibrahim described a funny buzzing sensation that developed over his leg wound shortly after his treatment. Laying his hand across the wound, he could feel a fast vibration, rhythmic and pulsing with electricity.

I nodded. "What about walking? Any pain in the leg?"

Yes. His leg became tired after only a brief walk, and the calf of the leg would ache until he stopped walking.

"When did the abdomen begin to swell?"

That started later, months after the injury. Now, after two years, it was getting hard to hide. He pulled his shirt out of the traditional cloth wrapped around his legs, the skirt-like garment worn by Somali men. A smooth mass bulged from somewhere deep in his abdomen, pushing up like a pregnancy.

Already I was formulating a diagnosis, at least a preliminary one.

I stood to examine him. A cantaloupe-sized mass occupied his lower abdomen, the top located at the level of his umbilicus. It was pulsatile, but different from an artery with a vibrating quality. Moving my fingers over the front of his left leg just below his abdomen, I could easily feel what the patient had described. He had what we call a "thrill."

In surgery, a thrill isn't an exciting event; it's the way we describe the electric feeling of turbulent blood flow beneath the skin that results from an abnormal connection between an artery and a vein.

I thought arteries were supposed to be connected to veins.

176

True, but not directly. Remember that arteries carry pulsatile blood away from the heart. Veins carry blood back to the heart. But before the blood goes back toward the heart, it travels through smaller and smaller arteries and finally through capillaries where the red blood cells have to line up in a row to get through one by one. Only then does the blood travel through larger and larger veins on its journey back toward the heart. So blood traveling in veins is usually slow and definitely not pulsating like in the arteries.

But something unusual happens if an abnormal connection is formed between a large artery and vein. The flow that normally heads downstream into smaller arteries is short-circuited straight from the artery into the lower pressure vein. This leads the vein to expand, and because the blood hasn't gone through the little capillaries, it is flowing fast, tumbling forward in a violent turbulence that leads to the sensation of the thrill.

I felt for pulses in Ibrahim's left foot. Nothing.

I nodded, understanding. The blood that was supposed to be getting to his foot was taking a shortcut, returning to his heart through a connection between an artery and vein, something we call a fistula.

How did that happen? The shrapnel had likely torn a hole through the femoral artery and vein, and when the body healed the wound (because of the absence of an adequate surgeon to repair the blood vessels), it joined the artery and vein in a healing union as complete as any marriage. So now as blood sped down the track toward the leg, most of it did a U-turn and headed back toward the heart as soon as it entered the upper leg. This left Ibrahim's lower leg and foot in a bad way, needing more blood. When he began to walk or exercise, the muscles of the leg would begin to demand more oxygen, which, because of the short-circuit, couldn't be delivered and left his leg weak and in pain.

So what was with the swelling in his abdomen?

I had my suspicions, which I would confirm with a special X-ray test. I sent him to Nairobi and saw him back in Kijabe the next week. It appeared that the abdominal swelling was a huge aneurysm of his iliac vein. The vein, normally content to carry low-pressure blood, had been subjected to the higher pressure of the artery downstream. In response, the wall of the vein expanded to form a kind of large balloon.

The problem with balloons is that they can pop.

Ibrahim was a walking time bomb.

What's this story have to do with bitterness?

I'm getting to that.

My underlying tenet is that God's gospel, the wonderful news that our debt has been paid independent of our deserving it, is evidence of grace. Grace, in turn, frames every interaction that God has with me. Anything I accomplish is by grace. As I was saved, so do I work. It's all by grace, and as the knowledge of God's grace for me begins to saturate every moment of my days and every area of my life, I begin to understand what walking in the Spirit is all about. My path is determined by love, not by law; by grace, not by the rulebook. All of life's daily disasters, I believe, can be traced back to the fact that I've slipped away from walking and rejoicing in the fullness of the life available to me on the basis of the good news. As I walk moment by moment in grace saturation, the natural outflow is grace to myself and others.

Unless something is short-circuiting the flow of grace.

Just as certainly as pride shuts us off from God's grace (not in reality, but in function, since we won't humble ourselves to ask for help), so bitterness shuts off the flow of grace to needy areas of our lives.

The Scripture uses the word "root" as a metaphor for bitterness: "Beware lest there be among you a root bearing poisonous and bitter fruit" (Deuteronomy 29:18). "See to it that no one fails to obtain the grace of God; that no 'root of bitterness' springs up and causes trouble, and by it many become defiled" (Hebrews 12:15).

When we see the urgency of walking each moment in grace awareness, the link between failing to obtain the grace of God and a root of bitterness takes on new importance. Calling bitterness a root is a particularly descriptive metaphor.

You can't see most roots. They are underground and unappreciated.

Roots are responsible for finding nourishment and water. Cut off the root, and the tree will dry up, *even in the presence of rain*.

Roots are responsible for stability in times of high wind and storm.

In most cases, if you see fruit, you can assume the roots are healthy.

Bitterness leads to a desert-dry life without joy. And what has led us into this desert?

The unwillingness to forgive a wrong. Or likely a perceived wrong. Anger is often vented in color with the volume turned up. Bitterness finds its vent in black and white. The volume is low. Background noise in a life of grayness without joy.

We plod through life, unable to enjoy the blessings of the next breath because bitterness is simmering, clouding our vision with dreams of revenge.

Beware the Sin of Pride

Choosing not to forgive is a decision to stand in judgment of another, a job that Scripture says is God's alone.

> Let all bitterness and wrath and anger and clamor and slander be put away from you, along with all malice. Be kind to one another, tenderhearted, forgiving one another, as God in Christ forgave you. (Ephesians 4:31–32)

Remember, we aren't called to be emotionless robots. It hurts to be hurt! Nonetheless, we are called to return love even when we've been wounded. And the source of love is our head, Jesus Christ. We take on the role as channel, not source. When Jesus informed his disciples to love, he used the strongest language possible. Not a suggestion, an idea, or a proposition, but a command. Love is to be the identifying quality to let the world know that we are followers of Jesus. So we are to forgive, not from our own strength, but "as God in Christ forgave you."

It's OK to say, "I can't do this."

That puts you exactly in the right place to receive grace!

Take a look around. Yes, we've been hurt, but we also have wounded others. Yes, the ground is level at the foot of the cross.

Perhaps we need to ask God to let us see the one who is the recipient of our bitterness as he sees them. They are also created in his image. And he loves them. Can we be so bold as to be bitter toward someone whom he loves?

But our old nature is bent around the law. We want to take names and take action! And, Lord, if we have to forgive, we want an exact number!

> Then Peter came up and said to him, "Lord, how often will my brother sin against me, and I forgive him? As many as seven times?" Jesus said to him, "I do not say to you seven times, but seventy times seven." (Matthew 18:21–22)

Why should we forgive?

I'll give you a selfish reason.

180

Because we are only hurting ourselves. While we coddle our bitter feelings, obsessing over past wrongs, our peace is destroyed, our sleep is robbed, and our health breaks down.

A benefit of a life lived in moment-by-moment trust is that wrongs tend to go unnoticed, falling from us like the proverbial water from a duck's back. The Bible says it this way:

> Blessed is the man who trusts in the Lord,
>   whose trust is the Lord.
> He is like a tree planted by water,
>   that sends out its roots by the stream,
> and does not fear when heat comes,
>   for its leaves remain green,
> and is not anxious in the year of drought,
>   for it does not cease to bear fruit. (Jeremiah 17:7–8)

The King James Version says it this way: ". . . shall not see when heat cometh." It's as if when we live our lives trusting God, there are times when we don't even notice the hardship of wrong.

How can I take offense if I realize that the sovereign Lord, the Creator of the universe and my loving Father, has allowed a situation to occur? Did he cause someone else to sin against us? Of course not. But he allowed it, didn't he? And so with the simple trust of a child, we understand that our Father has not turned away. He continues to love us and allows the circumstances in our lives that will enable the image of Christ to form within us.

Why did Jesus say seventy times seven? Perhaps he wanted us to become so practiced in forgiveness that it becomes reflexive.

Sometimes, in the face of a situation where we are the recipient of wrong, or even recurrent wrongs (four hundred and ninety times in a row!), we need to quickly turn to the ABCs of spiritual resuscitation to stay focused on the grace of God.

181

A. Acknowledge your need. *I can't do this on my own.*

B. Believe the gospel. *He has forgiven me. I can offer that same grace to others who have hurt me.* Remember, the essence of grace is forgiving someone *who doesn't deserve it.* Forgiving someone who earns it isn't grace; it's wages.

C. Communion. Take time to meditate on the truth of the gospel until the beauty of the cross impacts your soul like it did when you first realized its power.

Unfortunately, once bitterness has taken root, its poisonous fruit may be picked over and over. So over and over we need to turn to our Father and acknowledge our need of grace.

Ibrahim's leg needed a constant supply of oxygen, a condition hampered by the fistula in his thigh. In addition, the large venous aneurysm threatened to rupture, a situation that would almost certainly be fatal.

Is bitterness robbing you of necessary grace? Is it hiding beneath the surface, threatening to disrupt the abundant life you've been given at the cost of the cross?

It took me several hours of difficult dissection through scar tissue to identify and close the connection between Ibrahim's femoral artery and vein, and several more to remove the large aneurysm from his iliac vein. But once the fistula was repaired, a bounding pulse returned to his foot. It was complex and intricate work, but rewarded in the end with adequate blood and oxygen delivered to a starving foot!

A destruction of the root of bitterness is no less complex and intricate, but the rewards are huge. Grace again can touch the hidden areas of hurt.

Restoration is possible. Spiritual fruits of love, joy, and peace can be exchanged for poisonous, bitter fruit.

We can't do it. But Christ in us can. So go to the first aid cabinet. The solution is just inside:

> . . . bearing with one another and, if one has a complaint against another, forgiving each other; as the Lord has forgiven you, so you also must forgive. (Colossians 3:13)

> Beloved, never avenge yourselves, but leave it to the wrath of God, for it is written, "Vengeance is mine, I will repay, says the Lord." (Romans 12:19)

> Let love be genuine. Abhor what is evil; hold fast to what is good. Love one another with brotherly affection. Outdo one another in showing honor. (Romans 12:9–10)

> Finally, all of you, have unity of mind, sympathy, brotherly love, a tender heart, and a humble mind. Do not repay evil for evil or reviling for reviling, but on the contrary, bless, for to this you were called, that you may obtain a blessing. (1 Peter 3:8–9)

Only one more for now. God can replace a root of bitterness with a root of love:

> . . . so that Christ may dwell in your hearts through faith—that you, being rooted and grounded in love, may have strength to comprehend with all the saints what is the breadth and length and height and depth, and to know the love of Christ that surpasses knowledge, that you may be filled with all the fullness of God. (Ephesians 3:17–19)

16

FIRE-ESCAPE CHRISTIANITY

Domesticating Jesus by Living by My Rules

When the Son of Man comes in his glory, and all the angels with him, then he will sit on his glorious throne. Before him will be gathered all the nations, and he will separate people one from another as a shepherd separates the sheep from the goats. And he will place the sheep on his right, but the goats on the left. Then the King will say to those on his right, "Come, you who are blessed by my Father, inherit the kingdom prepared for you from the foundation of the world. For I was hungry, and you gave me food, I was thirsty, and you gave me drink, I was a stranger and you welcomed me, I was naked and you clothed me, I was sick and you visited me, I was in prison and you came to me." Then the righteous will answer him, saying "Lord, when did we see you hungry and feed you, or thirsty and give you drink? And when did we see you a stranger and welcome you, or naked and clothe you? And when did we see you sick or in prison and visit you?" And the King will answer them, "Truly, I say to you, as you did it to one of the least of these my brothers, you did it to me."

Then he will say to those on his left, "Depart from me, you cursed, into the eternal fire prepared for the devil and his angels. For I was hungry and you gave me no food, I was thirsty and you gave me no drink, I was a stranger and you did not welcome me, naked and you did not clothe me, sick and in prison and you did not visit me." Then they also will answer, saying, "Lord, when did we see you hungry or thirsty or a stranger or naked or sick or in prison, and did not minister to you?" Then he will answer them, saying, "Truly, I say to you, as you did not do it to one of the least of these, you did not do it to me." And these will go away into eternal punishment, but the righteous into eternal life. (Matthew 25:31–46)

This passage has always bothered me. I don't like the idea of people walking around thinking that they are sheep (Christians) and then finding out at the final judgment that they are really goats. Their whole life has been about a colossal delusion.

From this passage, we understand that this may not be an uncommon problem.

It is a problem compounded by promoting a gospel of a domesticated Savior, a Jesus who exists only to wash my sins away and not take his rightful place as Lord and King.

I want to tread gingerly here. I am not talking about a works gospel.

I am not here to stand in judgment of those who, like me, call themselves Christians. I believe God alone is the Judge, and he has reserved the end harvest to make the call. Remember the parable of the wheat and weeds? (See Matthew 13:24–30.) The implication is that there are weeds and wheat standing side by side in the same field and that it is not our job to separate them before the harvest.

That is not to say that we cannot have our private suspicions. Jesus tells us plainly that we *will know them by their fruit.*

> So, every healthy tree bears good fruit, but the diseased tree bears bad fruit. A healthy tree cannot bear bad fruit, nor can a diseased tree bear good fruit. Every tree that does not bear good fruit is cut down and thrown into the fire. Thus you will recognize them by their fruits. (Matthew 7:17–20)

The very next verse is telling—a warning that should prompt each of us to take a careful inward look.

> Not everyone who says to me, "Lord, Lord," will enter the kingdom of heaven, but the one who does the will of my Father who is in heaven. (Matthew 7:21)

So it is not our place to judge, but it is our place to rattle the cages of everyone who calls him or herself "Christian" with the warnings of Christ. There are false Christians among us. They may look Christian, act Christian, pray the right words, put money in the offering, and sing in the choir. They may appear righteous but be whitewashed tombs.

I believe that a dissection below the surface, in search of fruit, provides the evidence.

We've used Bob and Sally Christian as non-threatening examples to give us a segue into discussions about the ways we commonly domesticate Jesus. Bob serves as an example of people who think they are sheep but in actuality are goats. I'm using my fictional guy here because I'm not allowed to judge a real person!

I think this one is perhaps the biggest problematic area of all. It's big because it has affected so many. And it's big because here, I believe, salvation and eternal destiny are balanced at a tipping point.

I'm sure we all know "Christians" like Bob. They may or may not go to church on Sunday, but they live the way they want to live the rest of the week. They've taken the offer of salvation, believing that if they've prayed a simple prayer, they're "in." Nothing dethrones the idea that they are now "saved." Jesus exists for them simply to forgive their sins and to facilitate whatever life they want to live, free of eternal damnation. Imagine a Jesus domesticated, wearing an apron, following us around with a magic mop to wipe away any sin.

Jesus isn't invited to participate beyond offering a fire escape.

I've heard some preachers refer to "greasy grace," the concept that because of grace, we can now live like we want. After all, there's always forgiveness.

Foolishness! How can we treat with contempt that which was paid at extreme cost?

Contrary to this popular practice, grace is what allows us to follow the path of Christ in obedience and self-denial.

> For the grace of God has appeared, bringing salvation for all people, training us to renounce ungodliness and worldly passions, and to live self-controlled, upright, and godly lives in the present age, waiting for our blessed hope, the appearing of the glory of our great God and Savior Jesus Christ, who gave himself for us to redeem us from all lawlessness and to purify for himself a people for his own possession who are zealous for good works. (Titus 2:11–14)

Notice that Jesus didn't just come to redeem. He came to *purify*. Consider this passage from 1 Peter:

> Therefore, preparing your minds for action, and being sober-minded, set your hope fully on the grace that will be brought

to you at the revelation of Jesus Christ. As obedient children, do not be conformed to the passions of your former ignorance, but as he who called you is holy, you also be holy in all your conduct, since it is written, "You shall be holy, for I am holy." (1 Peter 1:13–16)

It is in the setting of our hope fully on grace that we find the strength to obey. We're back to the realization that our salvation is only by grace, and it is only in relying on Christ's strength, not ours, in the realization of our weakness and the provision of his grace that we can live a life in victory over sin that threatens to enslave us.

Paul has a visceral, immediate reaction to the idea that grace enables us to continue in a life of sin, a life where Jesus has been emasculated and domesticated to serve our sin-need.

What shall we say then? Are we to continue in sin that grace may abound? By no means! How can we who died to sin still live in it? (Romans 6:1–2)

I'm only attempting to restate that which has been made clear in the book of James. Christianity without works isn't real!

What good is it, my brothers, if someone says he has faith but does not have works? Can that faith save him? If a brother or sister is poorly clothed and lacking in daily food, and one of you says to them, "Go in peace, be warmed and filled," without giving them the things needed for the body, what good is that? So also faith by itself, if it does not have works, is dead.

But someone will say, "You have faith and I have works." Show me your faith apart from your works, and I will show you my faith by my works. You believe that God is one; you do well. Even the demons believe—and shudder! Do you want to be shown, you foolish person, that faith apart from works is useless? Was not Abraham our father justified by works when he offered up his son Isaac on the altar? You see that faith was active along with his works, and faith was completed by his works; and the Scripture was fulfilled that says, "Abraham believed God, and it was counted to him as righteousness"—and he was called a friend of God. You see that a person is justified by works and not by faith alone. And in the same way was not also Rahab the prostitute justified by works when she received the messengers and sent them out by another way? For as the body apart from the spirit is dead, so also faith apart from works is dead. (James 2:14–26)

All this is to say that Christianity without fruit isn't Christianity at all. It's a prop. A façade. And it gives the world the wrong idea about our faith. As a result, the name of Christ is blighted and Jesus looks weak in the eyes of the world.

I'd guess that to James, the phrase *nominal Christian* or *in-name-only Christian* would be tossed out as a synonym for *heathen*.

Do those around us look on and know that our faith is real? When they look at me, do they see love?

Beyond the people who have deluded themselves into a false belief that they are Christians, countless other Christians sporadically (all too frequently) relegate Jesus to this domesticated saving role.

How?

By quenching the gentle voice of the Spirit as he prompts them along a righteous path.

Just one little look won't hurt. I can always repent later.

Jesus has saved me. But he really can't be serious about all that talk about money.

Love my neighbor? He can't mean my neighbor.

190

We domesticate Christ anytime we resist the transformation of our hearts that he desires. We're thankful for the ticket out of hell, but we're not "all in" when it comes to following Christ in acts of sacrifice and love. In effect we're saying, "off limits" to the promptings of his Spirit.

Do I welcome Christ into my life for the benefit of salvation but wince when he nudges me toward personal sacrifice or service? Am I satisfied with forgiveness but hesitant to share the good news with others so as not to offend? Is this not akin to fencing in the Creator of Heaven and Earth?

Gospel Fallout

I'd like to conclude our time together with a bit of review by talking about something I call gospel fallout.

Let's think first about something less pleasant.

Nuclear fallout.

Increased rates of miscarriage, cancer, and genetic defects. Contamination of the food chain. In addition to the immediate and early deaths in the proximity of a nuclear explosion, the misery is compounded around the globe via the spread of radioactive dust.

You might imagine that the living may eventually envy the dead. Why? Because the original explosion is only the beginning of a cascade of problems.

As ripples in the surface of a pond spread away from the splash of a pebble, so the entire world would experience the effects of a nuclear exchange.

I'm stating the obvious for a reason.

Most of us have grown indifferent to the possibility of nuclear war. My generation has grown up with the threat, and most of us don't even want to think about it.

Unfortunately, some of us have grown indifferent to the concept of salvation. Yawn. Sure, I go to church. I'm going to heaven when I die. Now leave me alone, and let me concentrate on living my life *in the here and now.*

And so as we look around at the mainstream church, and we struggle to recognize the difference that the gospel has made, I can't help but question whether someone disarmed the bomb before the explosion. A life lived without gospel fallout is a life where Jesus has been domesticated into a lesser role.

A Christian life that doesn't look any different from anyone else's is as ludicrous as a nuclear disaster without fallout.

That doesn't mean that Christians don't struggle with the same issues as everyone else. If they didn't, there would be no need for this book or any other to help weary Christians along the path.

I've written this chapter to highlight the problem of fire-escape Christianity. Christianity sans fruit. Pseudo-Christianity. Christianity that may or may not be real at all (God is our judge). Certainly it is Christianity where Jesus has been domesticated into a saving role. He's been made small, and I get to relish in the freedom to be my own boss.

Gospel fallout is all about the abundant life that results from being a new creation. It's about a life radically transformed from the inside out, a life saved to the uttermost. It's the abundant life that Jesus talks about in John 10:10. It's what Paul refers to in his letter to Timothy as "truly life" (1 Timothy 6:19).

We can look back over this book to get an idea of what this life can look like. It's a life where Jesus is enthroned, not domesticated, a life where Jesus is treasured for all that he is and is trusted as all we need and becomes all we want. When we embrace the concept of the real Jesus, we move from:

Anxiety to serenity.
Anger to acceptance.
Discontentment to satisfaction.
Guilt to peace.
Discouragement to hope.
Addictions to walking in the Spirit.
Failure to victory over sin.
Bitterness to forgiveness.
Greed to generosity.
A fear of change to rest.
Dread of the future to joyful anticipation.
Pride to humility.

Short of defining gospel fallout by the symptoms, it remains a nebulous concept, kind of like a definition of radioactive dust without understanding the harm that can come from it.

Perhaps we should emphasize what it isn't. Fallout from the gospel shouldn't be confused with a pain-free life. Far from it! We have a Father who loves us enough to orchestrate circumstances designed for character growth, not a rose-petal-strewn path. Gospel fallout doesn't guarantee earthly riches. The economy of the gospel is never "Give so you will get." It's "Give because we got."

The life I'm referring to is a life Paul calls walking in the Spirit. I love Eugene Peterson's paraphrase:

This resurrection life you received from God is not a timid, grave-tending life. It's adventurously expectant, greeting God with a childlike "What's next, Papa?" God's Spirit touches our spirits and confirms who we really are. We know who he is, and we know who we are, Father and children. And we know we are going to get what's coming to us—an unbelievable inheritance! We go through exactly what Christ goes through. If we go through the hard times with him, then we're certainly going to go through the good times with him! (Romans 8:15–17, MSG)

This life in Christ or in the Spirit is characterized by Spirit-initiated fruit.

> But the fruit of the Spirit is love, joy, peace, patience, kindness, goodness, faithfulness, gentleness, self-control; against such things there is no law. (Galatians 5:22–23)

Our new life is no longer defined by our strength, but by his. It's a life where we recognize that we have been crucified with Christ, and now we find our new life in him. Our new life is defined by being "in Christ."

> *In him* we have redemption through his blood, the forgiveness of our trespasses, according to the riches of his grace, which he lavished upon us, in all wisdom and insight making known to us the mystery of his will, according to his purpose, which he set forth *in Christ* as a plan for the fullness of time, to unite all things *in him*, things in heaven and things on earth.
>
> *In him* we have obtained an inheritance, having been predestined according to the purpose of him who works all things according to the counsel of his will, so that we who were the first to hope in Christ might be to the praise of his glory. (Ephesians 1:7–12)

A life touched by the gospel of Christ is to be defined by *agape*, real, life-changing love.

> By this all people will know that you are my disciples, if you have love for one another. (John 13:35)

194

A life touched by gospel fallout is one in which our amazement at being so loved (John 3:16) flows over to touch the world. This love is to be the focus of hot pursuit.

> Pursue love. . . . (1 Corinthians 14:1)

The life of gospel fallout results from abiding "in Christ." This results in the fruit of the Spirit to the end that God receives glory.

> Abide in me, and I in you. As the branch cannot bear fruit by itself, unless it abides in the vine, neither can you, unless you abide in me. . . . By this my Father is glorified, that you bear much fruit and so prove to be my disciples. (John 15:4, 8)

Remember what I wrote back in the introduction about gospel debt? I want to risk redundancy here because the concept is so important. Gospel debt is when my soul is demanding payment, and the currency is grace. Gospel debt is when I'm living outside of gospel fallout. I've re-created the mighty, gracious, loving, all-powerful, and all-knowing Jesus into a salvation dispensary.

Look at these verses:

> But grow in grace and in the knowledge of our Lord and Savior Jesus Christ. (2 Peter 3:18)

> Serve one another, as good stewards of God's varied grace. (1 Peter 4:10)

> Through him we have also obtained access by faith into this grace in which we stand. (Romans 5:2)

195

Most of us give mental assent to the fact that we're saved by grace. But beyond that, grace remains a nebulous concept, much like kindness or the syrupy sweetness of a white-haired grandfather. But grace is the characteristic of God that guides his every action with his children. These verses say we are to grow in grace, serve in grace, and stand in grace. Other verses teach us that we can "nullify" grace (Galatians 2:21), fall from grace (Galatians 5:4), and "fail to obtain" grace (Hebrews 12:15). Elsewhere we learn that there are "immeasurable riches" of God's grace (Ephesians 2:7), and we can be "strengthened by grace" (Hebrews 13:9).

I believe the soul that is living in gospel fallout stands firm in the grace of God, and grace awareness is present moment by moment as a chief characteristic of the life we were intended to live.

Because of the gospel, I can live as a new creation, a child of God with full access into all of the privileges of sonship. I'm an heir. Heaven is my destination.

But the effect of the gospel isn't just for the next life. It's for right here and now. After all, what good is Christianity if it can't help me in life's daily disasters?

Is a life lived in gospel fallout a perfect life? A sinless life?

Of course not.

But remember, just as oxygen debt is a normal part of human experience, so also gospel debt will occasionally rob us of living in gospel fallout. With oxygen debt, physiologic compensations begin immediately to deliver the oxygen for which our bodies are starving. And the better physical shape a person is in, the faster the compensation can happen.

That's what this book has been about. Getting into shape so that compensation occurs rapidly. Exercised often, the ABCs of soul resuscitation can become nearly reflexive. If we can come to recognize the common ways we domesticate Christ in everyday action and attitude, we'll be one step closer to victory.

Perhaps on TV you've seen someone dressed in a hazmat suit, one of those big one-piece yellow raincoat-like jumpsuits that cover the entire body and protect the person from radioactive waste. Unfortunately, that's the way some Christians seem to be spending their time—moving through the Christian life insulated from any effect of the gospel on their here and now.

That's a pretty ridiculous notion, but too true. Maybe they've grown up in an anemic church, and they don't know any better. They've been led to believe that victory over sin is something for the by-and-by. That's an even crazier notion.

All it takes is regular, disciplined application of some general principles, time spent going over the gospel truths again and again. But please don't think a life lived in gospel fallout can be reduced to a few easy steps to sainthood. I'm trying hard not to make this difficult, but not to leave you with the impression that it's step one, two, three presto-chango either. The first step in the resuscitation should make this clear enough, but I want to close with it again just to drive the message home one more time. I have a need, and that need will be met first by my acknowledgment that I can't do it myself. Sanctification, the process of learning to live a life like Christ himself, is a work of the Holy Spirit. The ABCs should nudge us forward, remind us that it's his work, and provide an avenue for the change to occur.

The gospel changes everything. 24/7!

Here and now.

17

INCARNATION

The Most Amazing Domestication of All

IN THIS FINAL essay, I'd like to turn this concept completely around. There is an aspect of the domestication of Christ that is amazing and precious to the Christian. It's not when we're busy putting limits on our Savior. It's when he lovingly and willingly took on the limitations of human flesh. For us. For you and me. Undeserving sinners.

I believe that we domesticate Jesus when we treat him as if he exists to serve us and not vice versa.

But I also believe that he came into this world not to be served, but to serve. "The Son of Man came not to be served but to serve, and to give his life as a ransom for many" (Matthew 20:28).

Domesticated . . . in Order to Save

This willing domestication of his own divinity is vastly different from what I have been writing about. But it is this identification with our limitations in which we find a solution for our sinful

199

souls. It is this outrageous plan of salvation, this domestication of the Son of God, that has resulted in his present exaltation.

> Have this mind among yourselves, which is yours in Christ Jesus, who, though he was in the form of God, did not count equality with God a thing to be grasped, but made himself nothing, taking the form of a servant, being born in the likeness of men. And being found in human form, he humbled himself by becoming obedient to the point of death, even death on a cross. Therefore God has highly exalted him and bestowed on him the name that is above every name, so that at the name of Jesus every knee should bow, in heaven and on earth and under the earth, and every tongue confess that Jesus Christ is Lord, to the glory of God the Father. (Philippians 2:5–11)

Within this incarnation, we find a dichotomy that stretches man's ability to understand. Jesus was man. True. Jesus was God. Also true.

He domesticated himself in order to pay the price for our sin. In essence, he has domesticated himself to purchase our freedom from domestic chains. Of course, in phrasing it like this, I'm referring to our eventual glorification in heaven. Of note, it is also true that his domestication or incarnation stands as the purchase price of my lifelong desire to domesticate myself in his service.

Fewer images of the incarnated Christ are more precious to me than at the final Passover that Jesus shared with his disciples.

> Jesus, knowing that the Father had given all things into his hands, and that he had come from God and was going back to God, rose from supper. He laid aside his outer garments, and taking a towel, tied it around his waist. Then he poured water into a basin and began to wash the disciples' feet and to wipe them with the towel that was wrapped around him. (John 13:3–5)

What can be our response to such a King? Should we not lovingly and willingly give up everything for the One who gave up everything for us?

Should we not strive to fix our eyes upon him and meditate on him and on the glorious gospel plan that he authored for us?

Likewise, how can we, limited human beings such as we are, not impose limits on our image of the Almighty? Is this something we are prone to do because we are small?

At the same time, just because I'm prone to do something doesn't mean I shouldn't fight it.

A Final, Simple Look at Our Problem

As long we live on this side of Heaven, I think a full, true understanding of Jesus is impossible.

But that's not to say (as we've seen within these pages) that we shouldn't try to nudge our souls onward toward a fuller, more complete understanding of who he is.

Is it possible to stop domesticating Jesus?

Not completely.

But we can make progress. And I pray that this book can be one of the goads to keep my soul (and yours) more focused on the real Jesus and away from an inferior domesticated version.

From where I sit, I seem to need constant reminders. So I have been my own first audience. What I am telling you, I need to hear myself. Over and over.

The first thing is always the same, and it begins with the recognition of our problem. We have an ingrained tendency to bring down the Almighty. Not just in the big things, but in hundreds of small, common, day-to-day things, many of which we have touched on within these pages.

My heart goes out to every troubled Christian soul. Should you not use every episode of worry, discouragement, bitterness, greed, guilt, discontentment, anger, and fear to ask yourself, as I do, *What does this problem reveal about my image of Jesus?*

Am I experiencing salvation to the uttermost or some shadow gospel that reflects a lesser Jesus?

I've come to realize that my image of Jesus suffers not because of his greatness or sufficiency, but because of the assault of my own inadequacies, the world's influence, and distracting every-day circumstances. That's why I've put this down in writing. It's what I need to hear.

After recognition, a solution to the problem comes in two stages: elimination of the false image and replacing it with a long look at the real Jesus.

I suspect many of you have had unspoken doubts. *If Jesus is really God, if he is really the Creator of all that I see, why doesn't Christianity seem more effective? If an abundant life is really the birthright of the Christian, purchased by the cross, then where is the evidence in my own life? If Jesus is really so powerful, why doesn't he act in a mighty way in my life?*

The silent doubts are confirmed as we sit on pious benches in our gatherings, listening to abstract talk about a distant God. That's what's so amazing about the incarnation. Jesus has bridged the gap, and he isn't distant anymore.

This book has been about recognizing that the problem is on our end. Our lenses are smudged with the dirt of life, and they are soiled daily. We need constant reminders of the greatness of Jesus in order to keep the real Jesus in clear focus. We need to stay vigilant to assess the state of our own thinking and to recognize that living small lives of worry, guilt, and constant discouragement are silly when our hands are held by such a wonderful, gracious, and powerful Savior.

There is no magical one, two, three and I'm-now-living-in-an-elevated-state-of-mind solution to our problem. But we can make progress, and with the risk of oversimplification, I want to take a surgical approach here (surgeons like straightforward answers, helpful when you have to make on-the-spot, on-your-feet decisions). Step 1: Realize there is a problem. Let your silent doubts be known. You've certainly seen mine here. Step 2: Try to eliminate the false images of Christ to which our soul clings. This means using our frailties and sin as prompters to ask the right questions. *What does my present situation (anxiety, guilt, greed, etc.) say about my image of Jesus?* Step 3: Take a long look at what the Bible says about who Jesus really is and what his gospel has provided for us. Faced with the truth, we need to decide, *Am I going to believe what is written about Jesus? Or will I persist in living a life where my image of Jesus is a weak shadow of the real Savior?* Jesus, help our unbelief.

If you've seen your own problem in these pages, hide away and meditate on the Scripture promises that give us the answer. Jesus is big enough, powerful enough, knowledgeable enough, wise enough, and God enough to handle anything.

The quest is to truly *know* him. Nothing is worth more.

But whatever gain I had, I counted as loss for the sake of Christ. Indeed, I count everything as loss because of the surpassing worth of knowing Christ Jesus my Lord. For his sake I have suffered the loss of all things and count them as rubbish, in order that I may gain Christ and be found in him, not having a righteousness of my own that comes from the law, but that which comes through faith in Christ, the righteousness from God that depends on faith—that I may know him and the power of his resurrection, and may share his sufferings, becoming like him in his death. (Philippians 3:7–10)

Some of you may be wishing that I would conclude Bob and Sally's story and put a nice bow on the package of their problem. But because we've used Bob and Sally as windows into our own lives, the conclusion of their story is up to you.

Will Bob recognize that he has been treating the cross of Christ with contempt and embrace true faith? Will Sally open up to Bob and lay down her guilt?

Can Bob lay down his addictions and find his satisfaction in Christ? Will Sally trade discouragement for hope, forgiveness for bitterness?

Let's say the conclusion of the Christians' story mirrors your own.

Will you begin to recognize the ways in which you have placed limits on Jesus?

Can you use anxiety and guilt to prompt you to analyze your image of Christ and his gospel?

Will you go to the promises purchased by the cross on your behalf?

Are you willing to exchange his peace for your anxiety, calm for fear, satisfaction for greed, forgiveness for bitterness, acceptance for anger, and victory over habitual sin for addiction?

I believe the answer lies in taking a transforming look at the real Jesus.

> Therefore, since we are surrounded by so great a cloud of witnesses, let us also lay aside every weight, and sin which clings so closely, and let us run with endurance the race that is set before us, looking to Jesus, the founder and perfecter of our faith, who for the joy that was set before him endured the cross, despising the shame, and is seated at the right hand of the throne of God. (Hebrews 12:1–2)